VITAMINS
FOR THE
SOUL

Alan K. Scotland

Kingdom Publishers

Vitamins for the Soul
Real live Stories of Love and Wisdom, Revealing the Heart of God Toward our Humanity.
Copyright© Alan K. Scotland

All rights reserved. No part of this book may be reproduced in any form by photocopying or any electronic or mechanical means, including information storage or retrieval systems, without permission in writing from both the copyright owner and the publisher of the book. The right of Alan K. Scotland to be identified as the author of this work has been asserted by him in accordance with the Copyright, Designs and Patents Act 1988 and any subsequent amendments thereto.

A catalogue record for this book is available from the British Library.

All Scripture Quotations have been taken from the New Revised Standard Version of the Bible.

ISBN: 978-1-911697-02-2

1st Edition by Kingdom Publishers

Kingdom Publishers
London, UK.

You can purchase copies of this book from any leading bookstore or email **contact@kingdompublishers.co.uk**

> *The Lord will guide you always;*
> *He will satisfy your soul in times of drought*
> *and strengthen your bones; You will be like*
> *a well-watered garden, like a spring whose*
> *waters never fail.*
>
> (Isaiah 58:11)

Alan K. Scotland has been engaged in Christian ministry for over 50 years, spending most of his time working with church groups in the US, UK and throughout the world. He has helped many people facing personal difficulties, often when they had given up hope. It is his fervent wish to pass on their stories so that others may gain strength and find a way out of the prison of despair.

Foreword

It is a privilege to write a foreword for *Vitamins for the Soul*. I have known Alan Scotland as a friend for nearly 40 years. Alan has been in full time, church ministry for over 40 years, during which time he has become a pastor to many pastors. Before going into full time pastoral ministry, he pursued a short career in the medical profession as a nurse. During this time, he was awarded the gold medal by Mary Wilson (then Prime Minister's wife) for nursing at the hospital in Anfield, Liverpool.

One of the main emphases of Alan's church ministry has been his commitment and engagement with pastoral care for people of all backgrounds and with a variety of emotional and spiritual needs, some of those needs being very challenging. Drawing on both his medical experience, reliance on the Holy Spirit to provide discernment and informed by the clear teaching of God's Word, the Bible, Alan has helped countless people to overcome profound challenges over the years of his ministry. In *Vitamins for the Soul*, Alan provides a wide range of circumstances in which any of us can find ourselves. These include dealing with grief, anxiety, depression, despair, the need to find strength to face life and our need for love. Using stories drawn from his extensive experience and encounters in pastoral ministry, he addresses how people can be freed from these issues, to enjoy mental, emotional and spiritual wellbeing, instead of feeling isolated and alone.

The book contains short, interesting, and well-illustrated accounts, focusing on pertinent issues where we all may struggle. Alan provides keys which find their root in God's Word, the Bible, to enable people to become free and to live in freedom. It is a timely and helpful book, in an age where people are living increasingly stressful lives and are being bombarded by messages from all kinds of media, some of which are negative and unhelpful. This book is a good counter to such negative voices and will be of benefit to all who read it, be they Christians or anyone else who is open to the reality of there being a loving God who wants a relationship with us. I highly recommend *Vitamins for the Soul*: read and enjoy!

Ewen Robertson
Training Consultant with Lifelink-Global

Contents

Day 1	What can I do when grief overwhelms me?	11
Day 2	Who will be my witness?	13
Day 3	Who will hold me when I am fearful?	15
Day 4	What can I do when I feel anxious?	17
Day 5	How can I cope with losing so much?	19
Day 6	How can I deal with feeling unloved?	21
Day 7	What can I do when I feel in conflict with myself?	23
Day 8	How can I overcome my shame?	25
Day 9	When I am in despair where can I find hope?	27
Day 10	Why must I suffer?	29
Day 11	How can I keep going when I lose the will to go on?	31
Day 12	What do I do when I feel distant from God?	33
Day 13	How can I keep the balance of my mind in difficult circumstances?	35
Day 14	How do I know when God is speaking to me?	37
Day 15	How can I solve a problem when I don't have the means to do so?	39
Day 16	How can I find strength when I feel so discouraged?	41
Day 17	How can I rebuild my life when I lack self-belief?	43
Day 18	How can I survive the cruelty of others?	45
Day 19	How can I find my purpose?	47
Day 20	When I'm lost in the detail of living, how can I find the bigger picture?	49
Day 21	Where is my spiritual home?	51
Day 22	When do I have enough?	53
Day 23	How can I get rich?	55
Day 24	How do I find strength to fight?	57
Day 25	Do I deserve God's love?	59
Day 26	How do I know when God is with me?	61
Day 27	How can I keep my heart open to God?	63
Day 28	How can I run and not get tired?	65
Day 29	Where is my home?	67
Day 30	How can I make more of my life?	69
Day 31	How can I believe in what I cannot see?	71
Day 32	Why can't people see me for who I am?	73

Day 33	Does God want me to be perfect?	75
Day 34	Who am I?	77
Day 35	What can I do to make the world safer for our children?	79
Day 36	How can I stop feeling negative?	81
Day 37	What does the future hold for me?	83
Day 38	What can I do when I lose focus on what matters most?	85
Day 39	How can I forgive those who hurt me?	87
Day 40	What can I give to others when I can barely provide for my family?	89
Day 41	How much does God expect me to give?	91
Day 42	Where is God when I feel defeated?	93
Day 43	How can I get to know God better and gain wisdom and understanding?	95
Day 44	How can I stand strong when I feel weak?	97
Day 45	What can I really control?	99
Day 46	Who will carry me when I stumble?	101
Day 47	Should I ever give up?	103
Day 48	What is the secret of success?	105
Day 49	How can God love me when I feel so inadequate?	107
Day 50	How can I find true rest?	109
Day 51	What is wrong with taking revenge on those who hurt the ones I love?	111
Day 52	Where was God when I lost my unborn baby?	113

> *As they talked and discussed these things with each other, Jesus himself came up and walked alongside them.*
>
> (Luke 24:15)

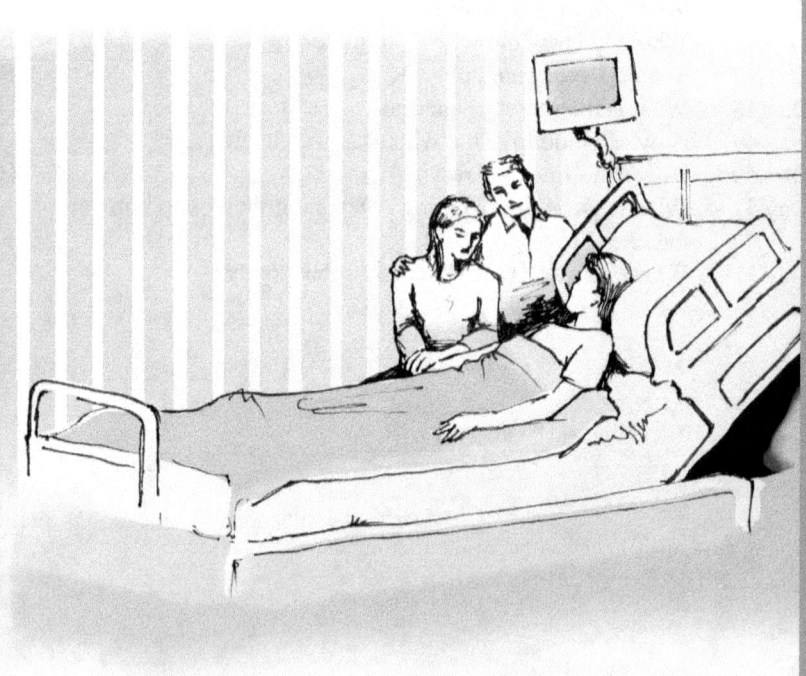

Day 1

What can I do when grief overwhelms me?

Each of us experiences the loss of those we love. When death comes, grief can overwhelm us. Longing for the person we have lost, we spend days and nights fearing that our suffering will last forever.

After Jesus' crucifixion, two disciples left Jerusalem on the road to Emmaus. A stranger joined them asking why their hearts were full of sadness and they told him what had happened. At supper that evening, the stranger revealed himself to be the risen Jesus and "their eyes were opened." (Luke 24:31)

Many years ago, a hospital consultant referred me to Lisa, a young girl of 15. Terminally ill, Lisa had just a few weeks to live and her parents were consumed with grief. I spent some time with Lisa, helping her untangle the deep bitterness that gripped her soul. Angry with her parents, she had distanced herself from their affection. She also judged herself harshly and felt overwhelmed by grief and anguish.

I prayed with her, and introduced her to Jesus as a friend who could bring her peace and set her free from pain. In tears, she prayed with me and the burden she carried was lifted.

Some months later, after she had passed on, I received a letter from her parents. They were astounded and grateful at the change in their daughter.

"You gave our daughter back to us," they wrote, "and the remainder of our time with her was beautiful and precious."

They were not religious people, yet they saw the transformation Jesus made in the final weeks of their daughter's life.

To lose a child is to suffer the worst loss imaginable. For many parents, it leads to a loss of hope for the future and that is the loss the disciples felt. Overwhelmed by the brutal reality of the crucifixion, they feared their grief would never end. That is why they left Jerusalem.

On the road to Emmaus, Jesus let them know he was with them and would always be by their side. With his love and God's grace there is not a dark night of the soul through which we cannot pass, renewed in faith and hope.

As long as I am in the world, I am the light of the world.

(John 9:5)

Day 2

Who will be my witness?

How many times have you felt truly listened to or heard?

Whenever I ask this question, the most common response is "I don't think I've ever felt truly listened to or heard."

Even at times of greatest distress, in sickness, loss or grief, many of us feel alone and abandoned. While many people choose to live or work alone, none of us would choose to face our most difficult moments without someone to hear us, to hold us, to bear witness to our suffering.

I'm reminded of the Jewish writer who found himself interned in a Nazi labour camp during the Second World War. Each day, as he went out to work accompanied by the sneers and aggression of his captors, one of the guard's Alsatian dogs barked playfully and leapt up to lick his hands and face. The dog did the same when the man returned, exhausted, at dusk.

After the war, the writer said, "it was my fellow men who took away my dignity and my humanity but a dog gave them back to me. That dog was my witness."

We all need someone to comfort us, to see and hear us, when we feel abandoned. A kind word, a touch, the barked greeting of a dog, can all heal our wounds. Yet all living things move on or pass away, leaving us to renew our sadness alone.

When Jesus said, "I am the light of the world," he did so after restoring sight to a man who had been blind from birth. Before healing him, Jesus said, "neither this man nor his parents sinned." I don't believe Jesus was being literal when he said this. Even the best people sin. What he meant was that everyone has eyes to see the love of God and that love will be their witness, in this life and the life to come.

> *The poor man cried and The Lord delivered him from all his fears.*
>
> (Psalm 34:6)

Day 3

Who will hold me when I am fearful?

We all know fear.

We fear for those we love, for our friends, our colleagues and for the well-being of those whose hand has guided us in times of crisis. We even fear love itself: the commitment we make to love and cherish until death is a reminder that we will, one day, lose everyone we love. They, in turn, live on in fear of the same loss.

We fear, too, our own failings, that we might not be as good as we would like to be. That was Jonathan's fear. A troubled man in his late 40s, he came to see me after his marriage had broken and he'd been made redundant.

"Perhaps I'm just not good enough," he said. "It's best if I never love again. I'm frightened of it."

I asked him if there was anything that might take that fear away.

"Yes," he replied, "If everything stayed as it was and didn't change. Then we would still be happily married like we were in the early years."

Each of our fears is, at its root, a fear of change and a fear of failure. When we are happy we want to hold the moment and never let it go. In sadness or in grief, we seek to recapture those moments. Yet they all pass, as they must.

The Psalmist understood this. What makes his words so powerful is that they are a personal testimony of his own deliverance from fear. Lost in the pain of fear and the troubles it brought him, he reached out to God and God answered him.

What is it, then, about God's love that delivers us from fear?

Whatever mistakes we make, whatever shortcomings we have, whatever losses we suffer, God's love is constant, it never changes. And when we draw near to His love, we have no need of fear.

> *Do not worry then, saying, 'What will we eat?' Or 'What will we drink?', or 'What will we wear for clothing?'*
>
> **(Matthew 6:31)**

Day 4

What can I do when I feel anxious?

Sometimes anxiety and worry can be helpful. They can alert us to real danger, remind us of our imperfections and drive us to make changes in our lives. But that is not how most of us experience anxiety.

For most of us, anxiety feels like a gnawing at our soul, a tension or nervousness which can appear suddenly, often without any specific cause. It can take over our lives, leaving us feeling panicked and helpless.

Reflecting on the many things he'd spent his life worrying about, Winston Churchill said, "I remember the story of the old man who said on his deathbed that he had had a lot of trouble in his life, most of which had never happened."

Margaret, a member of our Church in Essex came to see me, in a state of some distress.

"Every time I'm away from home, even if I'm just out for the evening with a friend, I know something bad is going to happen," she said.

When I asked what exactly was going to happen, all she could do was repeat that it was "something bad". She said it had reached the point where she'd avoid going out, then she added, "It's like I'm stuck in my head and everything's spinning. I don't feel grounded at all. Even when I attend Church, I always sit in the aisle, so I can get away quickly if panic overwhelms me."

I was reminded of the poet, Edmond Jabes, who said, "You think it is the bird that is free; you are deceived, it is the flower because the flower has roots."

Matthew tells us that God understands the anxiety that comes from rootlessness. Only a secure home can give us the feeling of being rooted in the world. It stops us being blown about like leaves in the wind.

Matthew tells us God understands we need food, water and clothing. He then reminds us not to worry about these things "but seek first his Kingdom and His righteousness and all these things will be added to you." (6:33)

When we experience God's love and the spiritual home He offers us, we find our deepest roots. We can then face our worries without being overwhelmed by them.

How I long for months gone by, for the days when God watched over me.

(Job 29:2)

Day 5

How can I cope with losing so much?

When we are prosperous, our finances in good health, our bills paid, our job secure, we look at the misfortune of others as if it will never happen to us. We may even judge others harshly for the losses they suffer, blaming them for their stupidity or lack of foresight.

Then the day arrives when misfortune comes to us.

We're made redundant, our business fails or we fall ill and, unable to work, our finances spiral out of control. We may be the victims of natural disasters, diseases or pandemics, which strike without warning and ruin our life's work.

This is the fate that Job, a pious, faithful man, suffered. Blessed with good fortune throughout his life, Job's faith was tested when his abundance was taken from him.

It reminds me of what happened to William. A stable, successful man, he found himself suffering inexplicable bouts of depression. As his mental health declined, his personality changed. Sunk into himself, he lost touch with his business and his family. Eventually he lost both.

With nothing left to live for, he came to me consumed by the unfairness of what he had suffered through no fault of his own.

William was a good man but that didn't protect him from the misfortune that must, at some point, strike us all. I told him about Harold Kushner, who wrote the famous book When Bad Things Happen to Good People. Kushner's son was born with a rare genetic illness and the book was an attempt to find meaning in that suffering.

Each of us will, at different times in our lives, suffer personal or financial loss. Like Job, we will be tempted to curse God, to blame Him for our misfortune or torment ourselves with the injustice of it all.

If this is the path we take, we will never recover, and we will live out our lives in bitterness and rage.

That is not what God wants for us. As losses overwhelmed him, Job lost sight of God's love to rediscover it and "repent in dust and ashes" (Job 42:6). Throughout his ordeal, even as he cursed the day he was born, Job never once cursed God. Steadfast in his love of the Lord, he went on to live a long and fruitful life, his fortunes restored.

Such a life is open to us all and when we are tested, we may hope that a part of our heart remains open to receive the blessings of the Lord, for God's love is with us even when we feel its absence.

> *And walk in love, just as Christ also loved you and gave himself up for us, as an offering and a sacrifice to God as a fragrant aroma.*
>
> **(Ephesians 5:2)**

Day 6

How can I deal with feeling unloved?

Few, if any of us, face life's challenges without wishing, at some point, that we had more love in our life.

Some of us face neglect or abuse from our parents or we find ourselves estranged from the love of our children. We may lose the love of our spouse or have to deal with emotional distress without a loving hand to guide us.

Often, our feeling of being unloved leads us to feel that we are unlovable. Lacking a sense of self-worth, we isolate ourselves from the world, where we fester or sink into deep sadness.

This is what happened to John.

An intelligent, charismatic man and a natural comedian, John was the life and soul of every Church gathering. Yet behind the clown's mask, he harboured a secret.

At 4 years of age, the people he believed to be his parents told him they were only his foster parents that he was not their real son and they could no longer keep him.

The next day he was taken away from the only place he called home.

Devastated and confused, John spent his childhood moving from one foster home to another. As he grew older, his clownish behaviour served to hide his shame at being unable to give or receive love. Locked in the prison of childhood neglect, anger and grief drive him deeper into himself.

Sensing his pain, I suggested he come to live with my family for a short while.

Our home was full of debate and occasional disagreements. One evening, we had a lively discussion. The following morning, John was quiet and unable to look me in the eye. When I asked him what was troubling him, he said he was frightened I would ask him to leave because he felt he'd expressed himself too forcefully.

"On the contrary," I replied, "You simply said what you felt and that's wonderful."

For the first time, John revealed who he was and found acceptance. In that moment, he felt, in his heart, that God did not create any of us to be bereft of love.

Through Jesus Christ, who gave his own life out of love, we learn the meaning of spiritual growth and maturity. He lived just 33 years among us, yet his love spread to all corners of the world and passed from one generation to the next.

However unworthy and unlovable we feel, whatever scars we carry through life, his love is always with us, even when we feel at our most desolate. It is through this love that we learn the meaning of redemption, in this life and the next.

Then Jacob was left alone and a man wrestled with him until daybreak.

(Genesis 32:24)

Day 7

What can I do when I feel in conflict with myself?

There are times in all our lives when we feel at odds with ourselves, when we feel we can take a number of different paths but are unsure, which is the best way forward.

Often these paths are not clearly visible to us. Rather, we are overwhelmed by a feeling of unease, that something has to change but we are not sure what. We may also be fearful of the hurt our decisions may cause others or anxious about what the future may hold for us.

This was the unease that Richard felt for many months before he spoke to me.

He was deeply unhappy in his personal and professional life and knew he had to make changes but, alone with his feelings, he had sunk into despair. His thoughts had become increasingly vague and confused. He'd reached the point where he was taking medication for anxiety and was barely able to work.

He said, "I just don't know what to do or what to think. I used to be so decisive and able to fix anything but I reached a crossroads in my life and it broke me. It was like I'd found a problem I couldn't name or solve."

Richard and I spoke a lot after that first meeting. Slowly, he began to let go of the belief he could fix every problem on his own and realised he needed God's help to change his life.

This was the problem that Jacob faced in the time leading up to his wrestling match with the stranger. The fight was long and evenly balanced until the man prevailed as dawn broke.

Prior to the struggle, Jacob had sent his family and servants away. Only when he was alone, did the man approach him. On his way to meet his brother Esau, whose birth right he had stolen, Jacob's life was at a crossroads. If he was to find the true meaning of his life, he couldn't find it on his own: he needed God's help.

The real wrestling match Jacob fought was with himself and he emerged transformed. The wrestling match was simply the means for him to learn that to grow, personally and spiritually, he had to surrender the illusion of self-sufficiency.

To find true direction in his life, Jacob had to submit to the will of God and face his own inadequacies. After all these years of struggle he finally came to terms with himself.

He learned, as we all can, that repentance is not without struggle but it rewards us with a life transformed by God's loving intervention.

> *For those who are according to the flesh, set their minds on the things of the flesh, but those who according to the Spirit, the things of the Spirit.*
>
> (Romans 8:5)

Day 8

How can I overcome my shame?

The difficulty of following a spiritual path is familiar to us all.

Our public persona does not always reflect the truth of our private lives. The conflict between spirit and flesh is a conflict between the person we aspire to be and the one we fear we are.

We may seek God but struggle to deal with our need for self-gratification. Unable to control our impulses we live in a state of what psychologists call "cognitive dissonance" – a conflict between two or more contradictory beliefs of behaviours.

The effect of this conflict can be devastating.

It is what Michael described when he told me he stopped going to Church. He said he felt unworthy before God because he spent as much time as he could gambling online.

While he hid his behaviour from his family, he couldn't hide it from himself.

"I lie to my wife," he said. "I have a credit card she knows nothing about and a bank account I transfer money into to pay my gambling debts. I make excuses why we can't afford to take the children on a family holiday. I feel ashamed of myself but I just can't stop."

As our conversation darkened, Michael told me had had suicidal thoughts because he didn't know how else to resolve the conflict within himself.

The American poet and philosopher, Ralph Waldo Emerson, wrote, "What lies behind us and what lies before us, are tiny matters to what lies within us."

This inner struggle is the essence of the journey towards God. We are imperfect beings and once we seek salvation through Jesus Christ, we have a loving hand to hold us when we falter.

Michael got caught in a loop of self-loathing and Jesus was his way out. Jesus gave his life for our frailties and he won't abandon us when we turn to him for help.

The apostle Paul was familiar in his own life with such frailties and he, too, overcame them by surrendering to God. He concludes Romans Chapter 8, "Nothing which appears to be good or nothing which appears to be evil, can separate us from the love of God."

That love saved Michael and it can save us all, regardless of the shame we feel. It is the bridge between the life of the flesh and the life of the spirit and we are all free to walk across it.

Now may the God of Hope fill you with all joy and peace in believing.

(Romans 15:13)

Day 9

When I am in despair where can I find hope?

There are times when we all lose hope.

In recent years, we have had to deal with the financial crash of 2008 and a global pandemic, which devastated many lives. Even without such large-scale events, our capacity to hope is constantly being tested.

When we lose a loved one, when our mental health declines or our physical health deteriorates through illness or old age, when our lives are subject to sudden unexpected shocks, all these can make us lose hope for ourselves and our future.

This is what happened to Wayne.

On a family boating holiday, his beautiful 7-year old daughter fell overboard. She wasn't wearing a life jacket and got caught on a branch which lay hidden under the water. In desperation, Wayne dived in after her but he couldn't save her.

Distraught at his loss and consumed with guilt, Wayne, who was a regular Church goer, was overwhelmed with grief.

"Why," he asked, "did this have to happen to us? Where were you, God, when my daughter was drowning?"

Wayne sunk into a deep depression. Unable to cope with the unfairness of what had happened, he felt as if he'd been cut away from the emotional and spiritual moorings to drift helplessly, buffeted in all directions.

"I lost the capacity to feel any joy in anything," he said, "and in the end, I lost all hope."

What drove Wayne to despair was the feeling that the old, familiar certainties of his life had been shattered. I said to him that all human endeavour results in loss: time moves on, circumstances change, our losses accumulate as those we love pass on. It is the nature of human life for that to happen.

The apostle Paul reminds us that a life lived in faith never loses its anchor. God's compassion for us never falters and belief in Him fills our hearts with joy that cannot be taken away.

Even in the most difficult times, He gives us hope rooted in the certainty of His love. Connecting with this love helped Wayne rediscover an inner peace he thought he had lost forever.

The blessings of the Holy Spirit turn despair into hope and that is the true joy of believing.

'Pardon me, my Lord', Gideon replied, 'but if the Lord is with us, why has all this happened to us?'

(Judges 6:13)

Day 10

Why must I suffer?

Making sense of suffering is one of the most difficult challenges we face.

When Gideon fled the Midianites and found himself hiding in a cave, fearing for his life and the lives of those he loved, he struggled to make sense of all the disasters that had befallen him. He couldn't understand why God had abandoned him.

Sometimes our suffering is so great that it strips our life of all meaning. The Holocaust survivor Primo Levi reached out of the window of his cell in the Auschwitz concentration came to grab in icicle to alleviate his thirst. As he touched it, a Nazi guard kicked it out of his hand. When Levi asked "Why?" the guard replied, "Here there is no why."

A loving mother of two daughters, Abigail would do anything to help other people, despite the fact that her own childhood was overshadowed by abuse and her youngest daughter, Anna, was gravely ill with a hole in her heart.

Abigail worked hard to raise the money for Anna to have an operation in Bordeaux. Things did not go well and Anna never recovered from the 12-hour surgery.

Consumed with grief, Abigail took an overdose.

My wife and I were called in to visit her and bring her home with us. That night she came to faith in Christ and a ray of hope shone in her heart.

Gideon and Abigail both sought an answer as to why they had to suffer as they did. It would have been understandable if they had let their suffering overwhelm them. Yet they did not.

Against the odds, Gideon went on to defeat the Midianites with an army of just 300 men and after her daughter died, Abigail found a connection to God. As time passed, her wounds healed and she remembered her daughter with love and joy instead of confusion and helplessness.

The path to God is not an easy one. It is only through conflict, through bad things happening to us, that we can be awakened from our complacency. We cannot solve life's problems on our own and an over-estimation of our own power is the path to self-destruction.

Inevitably we all suffer: it is a necessary part of every life. What God asks of us is that we respond to this suffering by rising above our circumstances, by becoming more than we are and the key to this growth is to dedicate ourselves to God.

In easing our pain, God is the antidote to the chaos of self-obsession.

> *But you, keep your head in all situations, endure hardship, do the work of an evangelist, discharge all the duties of your ministry.*
>
> (2 Timothy 4:5)

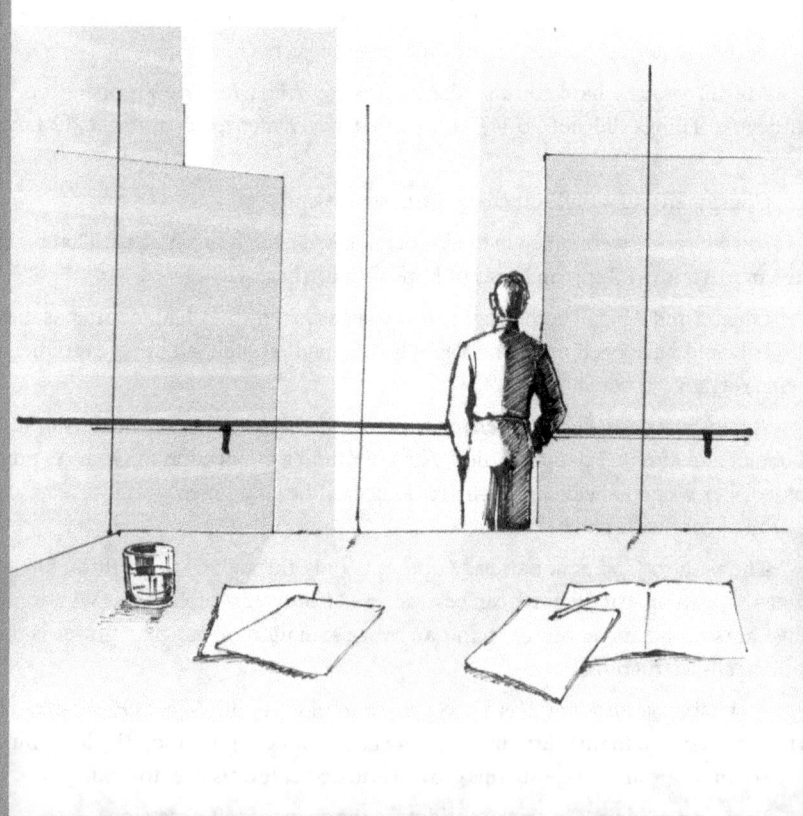

Day 11

How can I keep going when I lose the will to go on?

Often, what distinguishes success from failure, living our lives to their fullest potential from falling short, maintaining a constant connection to God from losing ourselves in the challenge of our daily lives, is persistence.

The film star Will Smith said, "You might have more talent than me, you might be smarter than me, you might be sexier than me. You might be all of those things. You got me in nine categories. But if we get on the treadmill together, there's two things: you're getting off first or I'm going to die. It's really that simple."

That capacity to persist, to refuse defeat on our path through life, distinguishes the lives of many extraordinary people. Yet it is a path few can sustain.

Eric was a man who pushed himself further than most. He worked hard at his business. Known for being first one into the office in the morning and last one out in the evening, he built a hugely successful company that employed more than 200 people. He'd overcome many challenges along the way but when his wife Shelley, who'd supported him on his journey, fell ill, he couldn't cope.

At first, he applied his formidable energy and considerable wealth to getting the best treatment for Shelley but as her health declined so did his will to carry on. For the first time in his life, he'd met a problem he couldn't solve.

In Second Timothy, the Apostle Paul's final epistle, he exhorts Timothy to "preach in season and out of season". He warns him to be prepared for the time "when people will not put up with sound doctrine", when they will take the easy path of listening only to teachers who confirm their prejudices.

At the end of his life, Paul is reminding Timothy of the necessity of persistence. All Christians face great challenges in living in the light of Christ just as Eric faced great challenges in coping with his wife's illness.

Life never goes to plan and we must all find the will to keep going when circumstances make it seem impossible. Eric found the will to persist by rediscovering his connection to God in the knowledge that God is with us, especially when the world turns against us.

Take the flour and bake twelve loaves of bread, using two-tenths of an ephah for each loaf.

(Leviticus 24:5)

Day 12

What do I do when I feel distant from God?

There are moments in our lives when our connection to God feels strong, when we go through our days energised by His presence and certain of our place in the plan He has for us.

Then there are days when we feel lost, disconnected from Him.

The Romantic poet William Wordsworth described this feeling in a famous poem:

> "The world is too much with us: late and soon,
> Getting and spending we lay waste our powers"

It's so easy to be overwhelmed by the pressures of living in the modern world with all its complexities. Often it feels as if we have no time for God and as we busy ourselves with keeping our heads above financial, physical or emotional problems, we lose sight of what matters most.

This was Eva's experience. A faithful and active member of our congregation, she confessed there were times when she felt detached from God's love. Concerned she was failing in her faith, she wanted to know how I kept the feeling of being close to God as I went about my life.

I answered her honestly and said there were times when I, too, lost sight of Him. I explained about times in my life when I was too distracted or distressed to notice Him.

"What, then, do you do?" she asked.

I thought for a moment and told her that I learned to trust in Him even when I cannot trace Him. His Word to me is as good as His presence. I kept praying until the feeling of His presence in my life returned.

We are, after all, imperfect beings and God understands that. And it's because of our imperfection that He keeps a loving eye on us. He knows we will lose sight of Him from time to time but He is steadfast where we are not.

In the Epistle to the Hebrews, Paul reminds us that God said, "I will never leave you nor forsake you" and that is the meaning of his command in Leviticus to "take the finest flour and bake twelve loaves of bread". The loaves represent the twelve tribes of Israel and He is teaching them this ritual as a reminder of His unlimited love and commitment.

There will be times when we all lose sight of this love, when we "lay waste our powers" and get lost in the labyrinth of our lives. But God's love is always with us and shines at its strongest when we are at our weakest.

For God has not given us a spirit of fear, but of power and love and of a sound mind.

(Timothy 1:7)

Day 13

How can I keep the balance of my mind in difficult circumstances?

Every one of us experiences moments when it feels like we are losing the balance of our mind: thoughts take on a life of their own and torment us, we feel sick with anxiety or our hearts tremble with fear.

When these feelings become difficult to shake off, we may ask our Doctor for medication or we may self-medicate with alcohol or drugs. That is not what God wants for us.

Eileen became fearful of going out after her husband died. If she found herself in company, her heart raced and she felt overwhelmed with fear. Yet if she stayed at home, she sunk into a deep sadness, often sitting in her chair or lying in bed, unable to move.

What made this particularly traumatic for her, was that she used to be a gregarious person, always out with friends or attending various meetings and gatherings.

She asked God for help but nothing changed.

What helped her rediscover her old self and move on with her life, was remembering who she was. Eileen didn't have to learn new skills or change her personality. She was good enough as she was – she'd just lost the connection with her own power. She now found the courage to share her heart and find encouragement, which gave her reassurance and the will to reconnect.

And that is the message of Paul's letter to Timothy, whom he'd brought into the Christian faith.

He reminded Timothy that his essence was not to be fearful or helpless. Rather, God made us all to be strong and powerful. The source of that strength was the love He has for us all and it's that love that restores the balance of our mind when we feel our lives spinning out of control.

Paul knew that Timothy, like all Christians, would face persecution. His faith would be challenged and there were many who would seek to silence him. Facing those challenges meant maintaining a sound mind and that is the same challenge Eileen faced.

Having lost her husband, the rock in her life, she lost sight of herself and it took God's love to light the path back to her true self and to cast out all fear.

> *The Lord came and stood there calling as at other times. 'Samuel! Samuel!' Then Samuel said, 'Speak Lord for your servant is listening.'*
>
> **(1 Samuel 3:10)**

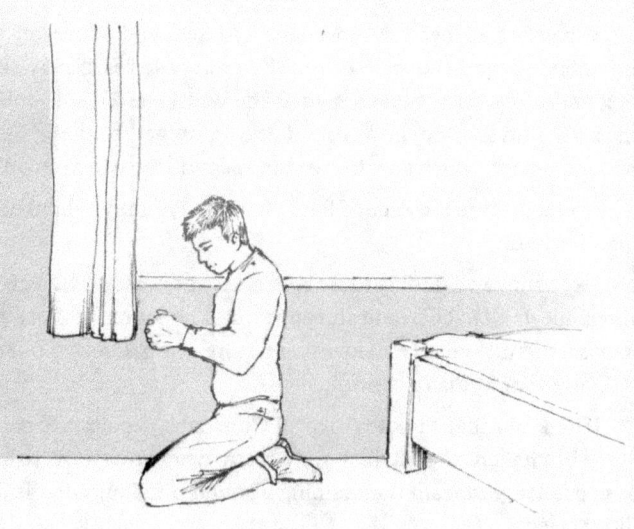

Day 14

How do I know when God is speaking to me?

Our lives are busy.

Lost in our busy lives, hearing voices tell us to do one thing then another, it is little surprise that when God speaks to us, we do not hear him or, if we do, we don't know how to respond.

That's what happened when God called out to Samuel while he was still a young boy. From birth Samuel was favoured by God and, as a man, he would anoint Saul and David, the first Kings of Israel. Yet when God called to awaken his heart, Samuel mistook God's voice for that of the High Priest Eli.

This happened three times before Eli realised it was God calling the young boy and the next time God called, Samuel replied, "Speak Lord for your servant is listening."

None of us know when or how God will call us. The most we can do is to be ready to hear Him when he does.

Robert told me about the moment God spoke to Him for the first time.

Brought up in a good family who were not churchgoers, his knowledge of the Bible came from Morning Assembly and mandatory Religious Education lessons at school.

One evening he was alone in his room when he heard a voice calling his name and felt a rush of love, deep in his heart. Before he knew what was happening, he fell to his knees and prayed.

Many years later, when describing that evening, he said, "I don't know why I prayed. I wasn't thinking about God and I certainly wasn't expecting Him to speak to me, a young boy who'd never opened a Bible outside of school. Don't ask me how, but I knew it was Him and from that moment, the course of my life was set."

Robert went on to become a church leader and his experience mirrors that of Samuel: God entered their hearts when they responded to His call with humility.

God showed patience with Samuel as He does with all of us. In the Epistle of James, the brother of Jesus writes to the early Christians, "Humble yourselves before the Lord and He will lift you up."

These are sentiments echoed by the boxer Mike Tyson, who, after living a troubled life and recovering from his addictions, said, "If you are not humble, humbleness will visit itself upon you."

That "visit", even if we experience it as the negative consequences of our arrogance, is the voice of God and we must be ready to receive it with a humble heart.

'Your servant has nothing there at all', she said,
'except a small jar of olive oil.'

(2 Kings 4:2)

Day 15

How can I solve a problem when I don't have the means to do so?

We sometimes find ourselves faced with a problem which, through no fault of our own, we are unable to solve.

This was the situation facing the woman in the Book of Kings. Her husband was dead and, to compound her misfortunes, his creditors were coming to her house to take her two boys as slaves.

Emma felt similarly helpless when, after a long illness, she lost her job and lost control of her finances. She fell into arrears on her mortgage. After repeatedly being unable to meet revised payment schedules, the bank was threatening to repossess her house.

When we talked about her situation, she felt at her lowest ebb. Her physical health had improved but she was in despair. She hadn't been able to find a job of anything like what she used to earn and she didn't have the means to pay her debts.

We talked about the woman whose story is told in 2 Kings. At her lowest ebb, with nothing to her name "except a small jar of olive oil", the woman asked the prophet Elisha for help. He told her to go to her neighbours and ask them for empty jars. He then instructed her to pour oil from her small jar until each of the jars was full. Miraculously, the jars filled with oil. Elisha then told her to sell the oil to pay the debts.

Elisha could have asked the woman to ask for full jars of oil, not empty ones or he could have chosen to fill the jars himself.

By asking the woman to pour the oil herself, he let feel, directly, the presence of God in her life. With every jar she filled, she felt His blessings pouring through her.

Emma wept and the feeling of helplessness was lifted from her shoulders. With renewed energy, she asked the bank for one more chance. Reluctantly, they agreed. Within two months, she had a new job. She worked hard and, with the love of God in her heart, she regained financial, emotional and spiritual balance in her life.

By receiving the small acts of faith we offer to Him, God multiplies our blessings: out of despair He delivers hope, out of poverty He delivers abundance.

> *Consider him who endured such opposition from sinners, so that you will not grow weary and lose heart.*
>
> (Hebrews 12:3)

Day 16

How can I find strength when I feel so discouraged?

There are many reasons for us to feel discouraged.

We face many challenges in our personal lives that often seem insurmountable. We may lose our job or find ourselves struggling with our physical or mental health.

Beyond ourselves, the wider world wrestles with increasingly intractable problems from the global pandemic to rising poverty and inequality.

Often, we are discouraged by a feeling of not being good enough, that we lack the ability or the wisdom of those around us. This is how Winston Churchill felt when he looked back on his early life. "I was," he said, "considerably discouraged by my school days…It is not pleasant to feel oneself so completely outclassed and left behind at the beginning of the race."

This is also how Julian felt. Less academically gifted than his older brother, he'd always felt he was playing catch up with a boy who was too quick for him. While his parents did their best to share their love equally, he knew they were disappointed in him.

"I was in no doubt," he said to me, "that I was the lesser brother."

These early experiences set up a pattern in Julian's life, where he found himself unable to stick with anything. He drifted from job to job and each time he failed at something, it deepened his sense of being a failure as a son, a brother and a husband.

The message Paul seeks to impart in his Epistle to the Hebrews, is that we must keep in mind the passion of Christ, "him who endured such opposition from sinners."

If, writes Paul, Jesus persevered through persecution without being overwhelmed by discouragement, then, through faith in God, we can all find encouragement, whatever our personal circumstances. As Churchill said, "success comes from going from failure to failure without loss of enthusiasm."

With a renewed sense of God's purpose for him, Julian discovered a resolve he never believed he had. Despite being in his late 30s, he retrained and went on to establish a successful career.

Through faith in God and by escaping from the prison of the self, we learn not to be discouraged by failure. Rather, we accept failure as a necessary part of every human life and we find the will to persevere in the strength we find in the Lord. In doing so, we lead a successful life, whatever misfortune we find along the way.

> *Come let us rebuild the walls of Jerusalem, and we will no longer be in disgrace.*
>
> (Nehemiah 2:17)

Day 17

How can I rebuild my life when I lack self-belief?

Many of us feel that we are not making the most of the gifts God has given us.

We feel we can do more but we lack the confidence to believe we can make a difference. Sometimes we just don't know which way to turn.

This was the problem June faced following the death of her husband. Having lost the love of her life, she wanted to become even more involved in the life of the church. However, in the weeks after her husband's death, it became apparent the family's finances were not what she believed them to be.

Unknown to her and their grow-up children, her husband had spent their savings and defaulted on loans he'd taken out to cover his losses. The credit agreements were in joint names as he'd asked June to sign the forms without fully explaining to her what the implications were.

June felt betrayed and her life began to fall apart. Having lost her husband, she now faced financial ruin and she fell into a deep depression.

Like Nehemiah, June faced seemingly insurmountable obstacles. Where Nehemiah had to rebuild the ruined city of Jerusalem, she had to rebuild her life. In both cases, the odds against success seemed immense. In both cases, the solution was the same.

Despite being ridiculed and facing hostility, Nehemiah rebuilt the walls of Jerusalem in just 52 days. He did it by enlisting the help of many people who shared his vision and who were inspired by his self-belief. Nehemiah knew he could not rebuild the walls of the city alone. It had to be a collective endeavour, led by the love and guidance of God.

Once the shock of her husband's dishonesty lessened, June rebuilt her life. Supported by friends, family and the Christian community, she gained the confidence to move on with her life. "I was a fool," she said, reflecting on the new life she'd built, "to think I could sort everything out myself. I needed other people and, above all, I needed God."

We are not made to live in isolation from God. Without seeing the depth of His care for us, we become isolated from Him and from those people who will be there for us in our hour of need, if only we have eyes to see them.

> *The hand of the Lord was on me, and He brought me out by the Spirit of the Lord, and he set me in the middle of the valley, it was full of bones.*
>
> (Ezekiel 37:1)

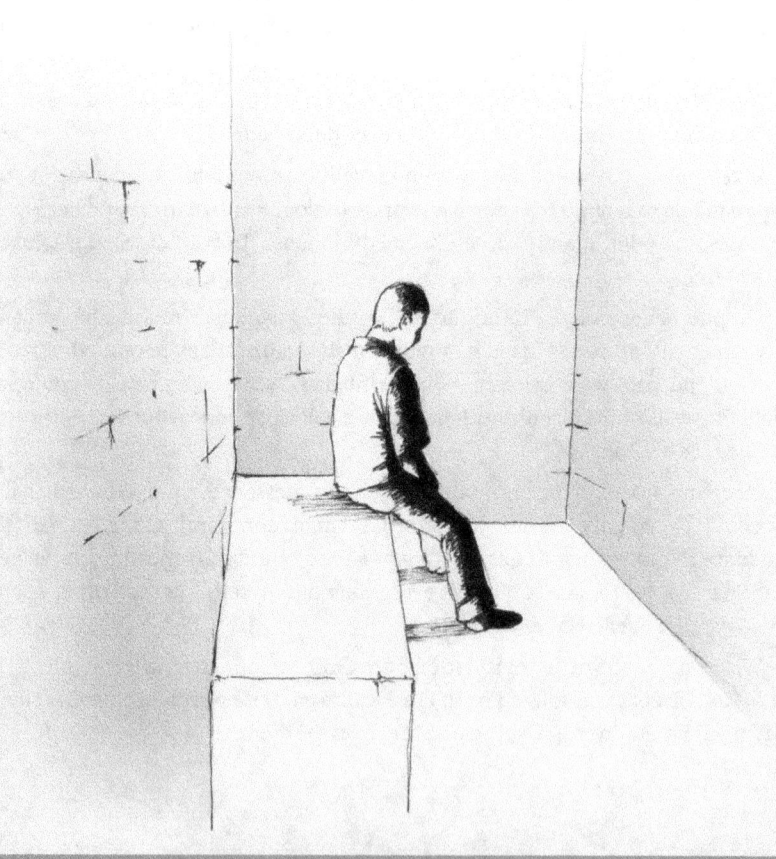

Day 18

How can I survive the cruelty of others?

Not one of us knows what will break our spirit until we are faced with a challenge so immense that we collapse under the pressure.

For some that challenge might be a sudden, unexpected loss. For others, it might be the horror of war. For Peter, a pastor in China, it was a long and brutal incarceration.

Peter was a kind, gentle man who devoted his life to God.

When he was arrested by the Chinese authorities for preaching the Gospel, he knew he would be punished. He had no idea how severe that punishment would be.

For 17 years, Peter was kept in solitary confinement. Every day, the routine was the same. He'd be sent into a sewer which he had to clean with his bare hands. The stench alone was unbearable. Back in his cell, the guards passed Peter his meagre rations on a large pole to avoid the toxic smell and risk of infection.

Miraculously, he survived and when he was released, I went to visit him secretly in Beijing, along with several other pastors.

When we asked him how he got through his ordeal, with tears in his eyes, he sang to us:

> "He walks with me and he talks with me
> And he tells me I am his all
> And there were things we shared
> As we tarried there
> That none other could ever know."

We wept as we listened.

The one who walked and talked with him was Jesus.

Every day, Peter told us, Jesus would come to him in his cell. "I never once felt alone, he said, "Because I knew Jesus was with me and he lifted me out of my despair."

When God took Ezekiel to the valley full of bones, he confronted the prophet with a lifeless landscape. He asked Ezekiel if the bones can be brought to life, to which Ezekiel replies that only God can know that.

Then, as Ezekiel looked out across the bleak valley, God gave life to the bones and "they stood up on their feet." (Ezekiel 37:10)

Finding life in death, hope in despair, is what Peter experienced in his cell. Jesus endured unimaginable cruelty for our benefit and when we suffer in turn, he is with us. He loved the exception not the rule. He lived among the poor, the dispossessed, the sick and the dying and there is no wound he cannot heal if our hearts are open to his presence.

> *I have brought you glory on earth by finishing the work you gave me to do.*
>
> (John 17:4)

Day 19

How can I find my purpose?

The writer Albert Camus said that "judging whether or not life is worth living is the fundamental question" we all have to answer. It is also the most difficult question anyone can ask us.

Finding meaning and purpose is our life's work. There are times when we feel we are living a meaningful, purpose-driven life only to find that circumstances change and we lose our way.

That is what happened to Lewis. A committed family man in his late 40s, he'd worked all his life at a car manufacturer. He'd risen through the ranks to become a Senior Manager when, unexpectedly, he was made redundant.

Shocked, he struggled to cope with being discarded. He felt robbed of the meaning his work had given him. As the main earner in the family, his life had structure and purpose. Faced with the reality that his wife Sarah was now the sole breadwinner and supporting him while he was out of work, he felt humiliated.

Depression gripped him and when I met him, Lewis was suicidal.

Many of us can identify with Lewis and the consequences of losing the work that makes our lives meaningful.

We often take for granted the work we do. Going to the office or the factory appears insignificant alongside loving our spouse, caring for our children or serving God. But that is not the case. If we are fortunate, we spend most of our adult lives at work and the work we do, to a large extent, defines us. It gives meaning to our lives.

The psychiatrist Victor Frankl survived being a prisoner in Auschwitz and when he was free, he sought meaning in his ordeal. This resulted in Man's Search for Meaning, the first of many books, in which he wrote that "suffering ceases to be suffering at the moment it finds a meaning, such as the meaning of a sacrifice."

And that is the meaning of Jesus' life. Through all the suffering he endured, he remained true to his purpose of "finishing the work" that his Father gave him to do. At the end of his life, knowing his work of salvation was accomplished, his last words on the Cross were: "It is finished."

Whether he was tempted by the Devil or tormented on the Cross, Jesus stayed true to his purpose.

In time, Lewis found renewed purpose and fulfilment in a new job. He emerged from his ordeal stronger and that is what Jesus calls us all to do: to live a meaningful life, to remain steadfast in our purpose, to work to the best of our ability, to be like a rock to our friends and family and to serve God in accordance with the gifts He has given us.

And Elisha prayed, 'Open his eyes, Lord, so that he may see.'

(2 Kings 6:17)

Day 20

When I'm lost in the detail of living, how can I see the bigger picture?

It's easy to get so immersed in the concerns of our daily lives that we lose sight of where our lives fit in the grand scheme of things.

When the prophet Elisha is confronted by his servant who wants to know what to do when the Syrian army besieges the city of Dothan, the prophet prays to God to open the servant's eyes so he can see beyond his fear.

This story reminds me of when I was a child and we lived next door to a wonderful gardener. One afternoon, when the man was old and did not have long to live, he showed me some techniques that make a garden beautiful.

He was a kind man and a skilful gardener who'd won awards at local Shows. I listened to him intently.

"You must always remember," he said as he cut dead leaves off a plant, "that great gardeners always make room for new life. If they didn't do that, there'd be no beauty in a garden."

Years later, as a young student at Bible College, my teacher took me to see a tree in the grounds of the College. He showed me a dead branch and asked me whether life or death was triumphing.

"Death," I replied.

"No," he said, "Life's winning." He showed me a few tiny buds on the branch and said, "Without those tiny buds of life pushing through the dead wood, there'd be no resurrection and the entire tree would die. It's always best to look beyond the obvious because that's where you'll find truth."

Seeing the bigger picture, the truth concealed by what our eyes can see, was the dilemma faced by the servant who spoke with Elisha. Once "the Lord opened the servant's eyes…he looked and saw the hills full of horses and chariots of fire all around Elisha." Armed with the truth of his circumstances, the servant was full of confidence and, when the Syrians attacked, they were defeated.

God wants us to know the true dimension in which we live and to see that dimension we must be curious and look beyond the obvious. Jesus is our guide in this. As the Gospels teach us, he asked 307 questions and answered just 3 of the 183 questions he was asked. If we are to experience the deep beauty of God's creation and feel the immense love that led Jesus to sacrifice himself for us, we must learn from his humility and lift our eyes beyond everyday concerns. Then we will see life in all its magnificent beauty and we will not remain victims of circumstance. We will be able to overcome every challenge we face.

For as often as you eat this bread and drink this cup, you proclaim the Lord's death until He comes.

(1 Corinthians 11:26)

Day 21

Where is my spiritual home?

All of us, at some point in our lives, will feel a sense of spiritual confusion. It may happen because we suffer a deep, personal loss or because we feel the world around us, mired in hatred and violence, is not a place we can call home.

As Christians, in a society increasingly distant from God, it's easy to feel cut off from our spiritual roots. All around us, we see the fruits of Christian civilisation in our chapels and churches, so many of which lie empty or struggle on with dwindling congregations. Daily, we hear stories and sayings from the Bible that have been cut off from their source.

"I feel lost," Judith said to me.

After a difficult period in her life, she'd felt increasingly isolated from the wider society of which she was a part. "I go to work, I come home but I don't feel nourished in my soul," she said. "It's like there's something missing. I feel out of place, like I belong somewhere else and I don't know what to do."

The French poet Charles Baudelaire described a swan that had escaped from its cage and "dragged his white plumage over the uneven ground…homesick for his fair native lake." That feeling of homesickness, that we are not in the place where we belong, is what Judith, and many others, feel.

Judith and I spoke about our Lord's Supper and the simple hospitality of Jesus who broke bread and drank wine, knowing he was about to die. There was no grandeur in the setting or in the food he and the disciples ate. Rather, the grandeur was within, as Jesus showed us how to make ourselves hospitable to God's love.

Realising what was missing in her life, Judith found her own way to God and that path is open to us all. Our spiritual home is inside us and when we host God in our hearts, we redeem our own lives and feel at home wherever we are. People find one another in family – take them out of loneliness.

> *You have sown much, but harvest little; you eat, but there is not enough to be satisfied; you drink, but there is not enough to become drunk; you put on clothing, but no one is warm enough; and he who earns, earns wages to put into a purse with holes.*
>
> (Haggai 1:6)

Day 22

When do I have enough?

In the early 1990s, a neuroscientist described a new social sickness as "information fatigue syndrome". If he was writing today, as we bend under the weight of unprecedented amounts of information, he'd have to replace "fatigue" with "exhaustion."

It's not just information that overwhelms us. Our attics are full of stuff we'll never use, our offices are overwhelmed with technology we never have the time to master and our days are spent surfing the internet for goods we don't need and can't afford.

When, then, do we have enough?

That was the question Ashley asked me when, after years of hard work, he sold his business.

Like many successful business owners, he'd put most of the profits back into the business and although he'd paid himself well, he now had more money than he'd ever dreamed of.

He did what many people in his position would do and went on a spending spree. A new car, lavish holidays and a new wardrobe of clothes were followed up with endless smaller purchases. Then he decided to take a year off and that's when his new reality struck him.

"I can afford anything I want," he said, "and everything's lost all its value."

Within three months he felt constantly tired and six months after selling his business, he couldn't get out of bed in the morning.

In pursuing his worldly dream, Ashely discovered he had a "purse with holes". He could buy what he wanted but nothing satisfied him and this is the message of the prophet Haggai.

If all we pursue is worldly wealth, we can never have enough. This is what Jesus meant when he said that "it is easier for a camel to go through the eye of a needle than for a rich man to enter the Kingdom of Heaven." Jesus wasn't against rich people. He was simply saying we need to understand true wealth, which is to be blessed by the Holy Spirit and to find purpose in serving God.

That is the purpose Ashley found and it gave his life renewed energy and purpose. Such spiritual wealth is boundless yet it satisfies us, every moment of our lives.

> *For where your treasure is, there your heart will be also.*
>
> (Luke 12:34)

Day 23

How can I get rich?

One of the spectacles of modern society is the parade of lottery winners before the television cameras. The bigger the win, the greater the spectacle and as we watch, perhaps with a tinge of envy, we imagine that if we won the lottery all our problems would be solved.

Yet, nothing is further from the truth as lottery winners themselves are quick to say. While money buys a degree of freedom, it won't free you from anxiety, fear or ill health. Often, money magnifies the problems we have as it did with Brendan.

While still a young man, Brendan had amassed considerable wealth. By any standards, he was a rich man. Yet as he wielded the power his wealth gave him, he felt his life was becoming increasingly empty.

Fighting back tears, he said, "On the outside I have everything people want but inside I'm dying."

Brendan's life lacked purpose. Wealth had corroded his soul and, as the playwright Oscar Wilde said, he knew "the price of everything and the value of nothing."

Psychologists have shown that our lives are enriched not by money but having a strong sense of purpose and by serving something greater than ourselves. Jesus tells us to "sell your possessions and give to charity" and "to make money belts which do not wear out". These "belts" are what Jesus calls our "unfailing treasure in heaven." (Luke 12:33).

Brendan, like so many of us, believed he was rich when his bank balance told him so. Only later, did he learn he'd been seeking the wrong treasure. As we lose our anchor in God and the blessings of the Holy Spirit, we drift aimlessly through life, hoping that money can make us happy.

While money will protect us from the ravages of material poverty, chasing money or having more money than we need, leaves our hearts vulnerable to spiritual destitution. When we live in the light of the Lord, we are rich beyond measure. Serving God brings meaning and purpose into our lives and through Him we serve others, so they may also feel His love.

After discovering his connection to God, Brendan said, "I feel alive again" and when Jesus asked his disciples to "consider the lilies, how they grow, they neither toil nor spin" he reminded them that "Solomon in all his glory was not arrayed like one of these" (Luke 12:27). Glory is to be found in God and not in the trophies of the world.

> *All those gathered here will know that it is not by sword or spear that Lord saves; for the battle is the Lord's and he will give all of you into our hands.*
>
> (1 Samuel 17:47)

Day 24

How do I find strength to fight?

There are many battles, some important, others trivial, that we get drawn into in the course of our lives. Some, such as battling a serious illness, carry a mortal risk. Many threaten our emotional well-being, our livelihood or our relationships with family or friends.

Each of the battles we fight takes a toll on our lives. Occasionally, we feel overwhelmed by the battles we have to fight, which was the case with Doreen.

"I feel I'm fighting on all fronts," she said. "I'm fighting to pay my bills, I'm fighting with my kids, I'm fighting anxiety. There seems no end to it and I don't know how much longer I can cope without throwing the towel in."

The dilemma she faced was how to know which battles to fight and to know who was on her side. The passage taken from 1 Samuel is spoken by David as he prepares to fight Goliath in one of the most famous Biblical battles.

David, armed with a sling and five stones, knows he is not the underdog that tradition has made him appear. The Book of Judges tells the story of "seven hundred chosen men" every one of them able to "sling stones at a hair breadth, and not miss" (Judges 20:16) and the Israeli General Moshe Dayan said that David knew "how to exploit a weapon by which a feeble person could seize the advantage and become stronger."

But there was one thing, above all others, that gave David strength as he went into battle: his faith in God who doesn't triumph by "sword or spear". God delivers victory to those who choose their battles wisely and fight them in faith.

This is what I said to Doreen and, in time, she found renewed strength in God. This allowed her to put her own struggles in perspective, which made them easier for her to deal with. Above all, she learned that only when we surrender ourselves to God do we find the strength to fight with a balanced mind and a heart blessed by the Holy Spirit.

> *Sow righteousness for yourselves, reap the fruit of unfailing love, and break up your unplowed ground; for it is time to seek the Lord, until He comes and shows His righteousness upon you.*
>
> (Hosea 10:12)

Day 25

Do I deserve God's love?

Many of us find it easier to give than to receive love. It may be because we feel we are unlovable or because we fear getting hurt by sharing our hearts with another person. We may also believe it's selfish to want to be loved.

At the root of these feelings is a fear that we don't deserve to be loved. "It's strange," Elinor said to me one day after a church service, "but I find it hard to believe my family when they say they love me. I say to myself, 'What have I done to deserve that?' so I'm constantly working harder to please them. If I carry on like this, I'll wear myself out."

Even when love is offered to us, we feel we have to work harder simply to receive what we have already been given. This is what makes it so difficult for us to act on the words of the prophet Hosea and **"reap the fruit of unfailing love"**.

If we find it hard to believe we have earned the love we receive from those around us, how much harder is it to receive the love of God?

In sacrificing his life to redeem our sins, Jesus showed love that no human being deserved. Not a single one of us is good enough to be worthy of that love and yet it was given freely.

What Jesus wanted us to learn through his sacrifice was the virtue of humility. It takes humility to let ourselves be loved. When we feel unworthy and our spouse, friend or family member shows us love, it is incumbent on us to receive that love in good faith and with a humble heart.

We must, as Hosea urges us, "sow righteousness:" and "seek the Lord" in the knowledge that we can never deserve or earn God's love. That's why He sent His son to redeem us: Jesus suffered for us, not because we deserve it, but because we don't, not because we've earned it, but because we can't.

If the magnitude of his sacrifice can't be repaid, it can, at the very least, be received with gratitude and humility: a gift in return for a gift.

> *I sought the Lord, and He answered me;*
> *He delivered me from all my fears.*
>
> **(Psalm 34:6)**

Day 26

How do I know when God is with me?

The words of Psalm 34 are spoken by David after he fled from Saul and sought refuge in a cave. Frightened and desperate, he needed to know that God was with him and we can all identify with that need.

We stand by, helpless, as the world suffers from plague, war and all manner of injustice. In our personal lives, we all suffer loss and bad things happen to everyone, whether we deserve it or not. It's natural, therefore, to ask: where is God when we suffer? Why was He not with me?

I've spent my life serving God and doing what I can to alleviate suffering in His name. I've watched good people suffer from violence and abuse of all kinds. I've listened as people unburdened their hearts of the grief they'd carried for years.

Through all this I faced a choice: to focus on the negative, to allow myself to be overwhelmed by the enormity of human suffering or to find goodness and hope, in spite of all the pain.

This was the choice David faced as he sat in the cave and he chose to see that God was with him.

The philosopher Plato imagined a cave where prisoners were chained and, unable to move their heads, saw only shadows on the wall of the cave. They believed these shadows were real until one of the prisoners was released and able to see the fire behind him that cast the shadows. As he climbed up the cave, he soon realised that the fire was not reality either and only when he reached the cave entrance and saw the light of the sun, did he see the truth.

In his darkest moments, trapped in a cave, David's profound belief in God helped David overcome his fear. He was not in denial of his difficulties yet he drew deep on the reality of God.

Jesus said, "I am the light of the world. Whoever follows me will never walk in darkness, but will have the light of life." (John 8:12). "I have come into the world as light," he said, "so that no one who believes in me should stay in darkness." (John 12:46).

Jesus died to teach us there is redemption in suffering and through all the trauma I've witnessed, God's love has been the light that shines through all the darkness and the darker it gets, the brighter it shines.

They still did not understand from Scripture that Jesus had to rise from the dead.

(John 20:9)

Day 27

How can I keep my heart open to God?

Our minds are programmed to assume that the way the world is today will be how it will be tomorrow. It's this consistency that makes it possible for us to make plans and believe our children have a future.

However, this habitual way of thinking can prevent us seeing something unfamiliar or even believing it's possible. Because his customers were unable to conceive of mass-produced cars before he invented them, Henry Ford is supposed to have said, "If I had asked people what they wanted they would have said faster horses."

This struggle with absorbing the unfamiliar is what happened to June when her husband died in an accident at a young age. All her plans were thrown into confusion.

"It's as if I was living in one world," she said, "and then, in the blink of an eye, I was living in another. It was like a hole had opened up under my feet and swallowed me."

All of us who have lost a person dear to us, even if it's expected after a long illness, will know the feeling of stepping into an unfamiliar world and having to learn to live again.

It's easy to understand, therefore, how confusing it must have been for the disciples who entered Jesus' tomb and found it empty. Because no-one had ever been resurrected before, they assumed that Jesus' body must have been moved by human hands.

If it's hard to deal with the unfamiliarity of loss, which we all experience, imagine how much more difficult it must have been for the disciples to even comprehend that Jesus had risen from the dead. There is nothing, in all of human history, more unfamiliar than that.

In the Gospel of John, Mary Magdalene, stricken with grief, says to a man she believes to be a gardener who has taken the body of Jesus from the tomb, "Tell me where you have taken him." (John 20:15) Only when Jesus calls out her name does she recognise him.

> *But those who hope in the Lord will renew their strength. They will soar on wings like eagles; they will run not grow weary; they will walk and not be faint.*
>
> (Isaiah 40:31)

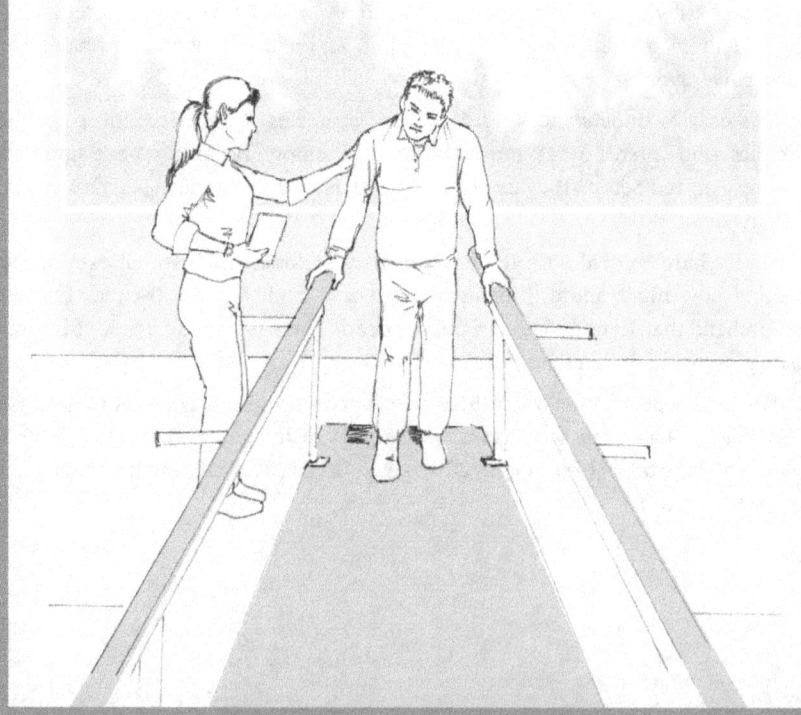

Day 28

How can I run and not get tired?

After a long period of slavery and exile, it would have been understandable if the prophet Isaiah had lost faith in God.

How many of us feel our faith falter when bad things happen to us for no reason? Or when those we love, suffer through no fault of their own?

This is what happened to Kevin, a young, successful businessman, who suffered a stroke.

He'd made his money selling religious icons and although he and I had theological differences, we connected beautifully as human beings. When I first saw him, this dynamic young man had lost the power of speech, could barely walk and the entire left side of his body was weakened.

Over a period of three months, he recovered well. He was able to speak and walk and the weakness that plagued him had all but disappeared.

Yet, Kevin was not well.

The stroke had left him spiritually weakened and he'd lost the will to carry on.

Within a few weeks, he was dead.

Regardless of our physical health, we can become spiritually depleted and weariness of the soul can kill us. At times, it can feel so exhausting to live, it seems easier to lose hope and give up.

Shortly before his death, the physician and athlete George Sheehan wrote a book about his passion for running. "Eventually," he wrote, "you learn that the competition is against the little voice inside you that wants you to quit."

It's not just for runners that the mental battle is more critical than the physical one. Isaiah, too, must have heard such a voice yet he found strength in God and was able "run and not grow weary."

Life is hard, yet our burdens are lifted when we live in faith. With God alongside us, we can persist where others falter, persevere where others give up and maintain our spiritual strength when faced with any manner of injustice.

> *But the Pharisees and the teachers of law muttered, 'This man welcomes sinners and eats with them.'*
>
> (Luke 15:2)

Day 29

Where is my home?

The feeling of 'home', a place where we can grow roots, is fundamental to our sense of well-being.

But where is our home? Is it a physical place such as a house, village, town, city or country? Or is it a sense of 'being at home with myself', of being comfortable with who I am, irrespective of where I live or the community of which I'm a part?

Feeling a sense of belonging is not easy as John knew from bitter experience.

Abandoned as a child, he grew up moving between foster homes. He never lasted more than a year with any family as his behaviour became increasingly destructive. In his teenage years he began taking drugs and eventually found himself in prison after he was convicted of burglary and assault.

Jesus would have understood the challenges John faced. But for Jesus, understanding was never enough: it was action that mattered. Jesus would have taken the time to speak with John, eat with him, help him. "There will be more rejoicing in heaven," Jesus said, "over one sinner who repents than over ninety-nine righteous persons who do not need to repent." (Luke 15:7)

If we are to find our home in God, we have to repent and it's never easy to admit our failings. It's far easier to blame others and this impulse to amplify our sense of being a victim gives rise to what Douglas Murray calls "the madness of crowds" where, in the name of social justice, we blame anyone but ourselves for our troubles.

The difference between a "crowd" or a "mob" and a community, is the difference between a place where unfashionable views are silenced and one where the wounded human heart is supported on its journey to salvation.

Of course, Jesus understood that people face enormous disadvantages in life and wherever the challenge was greatest, that's where Jesus went. That's why he spent his time with "sinners", so they might find their way to God.

And John eventually turned his life around by finding a personal connection to God but to sustain that connection he needed a community of believers to hold him when he faltered.

This relationship between self, God and community is what Jesus meant by 'home'.

> 'Can I not do with you, Israel, as this potter does?' declares the Lord, 'Like clay in the hand of the potter, so are you in my hand, Israel.'
>
> (Jeremiah 18:6)

Day 30

How can I make more of my life?

One of life's tasks is to make the most of the gifts God has given us. Like the movement of the potter's wheel, our lives turn as one day passes to the next, often leaving us feeling we have let ourselves down or failed to fulfil our potential.

What psychologists call the 'mid-life crisis' is the culmination of these feelings, and that's how Marc felt when he reached his 50th birthday.

"People talk about the house feeling empty when the children grow up and leave but that's only part of the story. When our youngest child left to go to college, the emptiness wasn't outside me. I felt it in my heart like an ache, a sense of hopelessness that wouldn't go away. I felt I'd never done the things I wanted to do."

We can all, to some degree, identify with that feeling and it becomes toxic when we look for fulfilment in places where it can never be found.

In summoning him to the potter's house to watch the skilled craftsman at work, God is reminding Jeremiah that living a creative, meaningful life means breaking our routines and being open to possibilities that we hadn't considered.

The potter also teaches Jeremiah, the importance of hard work. A skill isn't learned overnight. It takes time, patience and dedication. We can admire the work of great artists and craftsmen, but what we don't see are the years of hard work that made it possible.

The inventor James Dyson said, "I made 5,127 prototypes of my vacuum before I got it right. There were 5,126 failures. But I learned from each one. That's how I came up with a solution. So, I don't mind failure."

However, the deeper message that God is giving Jeremiah is that God's creativity far surpasses that of men and women. Whilst we may acquire, like James Dyson, vast fortunes through our creativity, only God can give us salvation and eternal life.

It is from God's perspective, then, that we must see the potter's wheel. His creativity, patience and dedication to us is boundless. Whatever we feel about success or failure in this life, God offers us more than we can ever imagine if only we do the work of seeking.

As time passed, Marc came to see that his greatest achievement was his faith. Even the most apparently successful people can feel like underachievers because without God, nothing human beings do can ever be enough to fill the hole in our hearts.

> *Now faith is confidence in what we hope for and assurance about what we do not see.*
>
> (Hebrews 11:1)

Day 31

How can I believe in what I cannot see?

We can all become disheartened. The visible miseries of the world can feel so present and the love of God so distant.

I am often asked how I keep my faith steadfast in the face of so much injustice. There are, of course, moments when I struggle to find Him but I never lose faith that He is there. And that is the definition of faith: to take the difficult path, to believe what others may struggle to see.

That faith defined the life of Eric Liddell who won Gold in the 400m at the Paris Olympics in 1924. He was meant to run in the 100m but since the heats were on a Sunday, he refused to run and chose the 400m instead.

After the Olympics, he went to work as a Christian missionary in China and his remarkable story was immortalised in the film Chariots of Fire.

The film won an Oscar but that, along with his Gold medal, would have mattered much less to Eric than his work as a missionary.

Years after his Olympic success, he said that "people who do not know the Lord ask why in the world we waste our lives as missionaries. They forget that they too are expending their lives...and when the bubble has burst they will have nothing of eternal significance to show for the years they have wasted."

The challenge God gives us all is to become aware of His love and that He is asking us to put the glories of the world in their proper place. He knows this is not an easy path to take, as it's only human to be seduced by success.

The fundamental choice, however, is what or whom we choose to guide us and Eric knew that "if you are not guided by God, then you will be guided by someone or something else."

God is asking to let Him guide us even when His presence seems less visible to us than the trinkets of the world. The rewards, as Eric Liddell knew, are eternal life and the salvation of our soul. And there is no greater reward than that and no greater waste than failing to see the Truth radiating through the worldly ambition of our lives.

> *But the Lord said to Samuel, 'Do not consider his appearance or his height, for I have rejected him. The Lord does not look at the things people look at. People look at the outward appearance, but the Lord looks at the heart.'*
>
> (1 Samuel: 7)

Day 32

Why can't people see me for who I am?

We all face times when we feel our efforts are being unrecognised and our intentions misunderstood.

This was the experience of Pastor Jim. After leading a church for many years, his congregation began to dwindle. As the number of people leaving reached more than 50, he discovered the reason for their departure was the new programme he had introduced. He felt deeply discouraged. He found it difficult to explain to himself how his intentions had been so misunderstood and he needed reassurance to overcome the loss.

"All I was doing," he said, "was being true to what I believe to be the Word of God. I want the best for everyone and I don't understand why people can't see that my intentions are good?"

This is the dilemma Samuel faced when God told him that he must not anoint Saul as King of Israel. Although he had already prophesied to Saul that he would not become King, Samuel did not know where to go to find the person God wanted him to anoint. Like Pastor Jim, Samuel was confused and discouraged.

I suggested to Pastor Jim that it is only human for us to misunderstand each other. We can't see into each other's hearts, so we make assumptions and often those assumptions are wrong. Our errancy, however, can, as with Pastor Jim, lead to harsh and unfair judgements. It can blind us to the path we need to take.

The solution is to trust that God sees is for who we are. For Samuel and Pastor Jim, trusting God was their way out of the pain of uncertainty. Pastor Jim thought he was doing what God wanted and he was abandoned by the faithful. Samuel sought to anoint a King and his search made him fearful and he felt lost.

In the end, they both came to the right conclusion: Samuel anointed David and Pastor Jim reviewed the changes he had made. This allowed him to reconnect to his congregation and serve another decade before retiring. To this day, the church remains a success.

Even prophets and leaders can be discouraged but to God what matters most is what only He sees, which is the faith in our hearts.

> *Then he said to them all: 'Whoever wants to be my disciple must deny themselves and take up their cross daily and follow me.'*
>
> (Luke 9:23)

Day 33

Does God want me to be perfect?

There are many demands made on us, every day of our lives.

We are expected to be kind and compassionate to those we love, competent and professional in our work, diligent and committed in our faith.

Sometimes, the pressure is too much and it takes a toll on our physical and mental health. This was the case with Helen who made a plea for help when she collapsed from the stress of meeting the many demands made on her time.

"I never felt I had a moment to myself. I was busy at work, then looking after my husband who had health problems and also bringing up two kids. But the real problem was my attitude. I didn't just have to juggle all those demands made on me. I had to do everything perfectly."

But isn't that what God demands of us? Doesn't he want us to be perfect in our devotion to Him?

It's understandable for us to think that but the truth is very different. Of course, living a life of faith isn't easy, which is why Jesus asked his disciples to "take up their cross daily." And Jesus himself showed the depth of his commitment to God and to us by sacrificing his own life.

There is, however, a vast difference between giving everything we have for God and being perfect in our lives and our devotion. It was because of our imperfection that Jesus came to save us. If we had any hope of finding perfection on earth, what need would there have been for his sacrifice?

What God asks of us is to persevere, to withstand the many injustices and judgements we face on our journey of faith, to act selflessly and invest ourselves fully in serving God.

Our highest aim is to not be perfect. It is to be good enough. Perfection is reserved for God and if, in this life, we can travel a short distance towards that perfection that we will have lived our lives well and He will reward us with eternal life.

> *You have searched me, Lord, and you know me.*
>
> **(Psalm 139:1)**

Day 34

Who am I?

In the modern world, it is fashionable to claim to know who we are. Barely a day goes by when we don't see people anchoring their identity to one group or another. We may identify with groups based on sex, race, class or a kaleidoscope of alternatives and say, 'This is who I am!'

The problem is that such identities rarely give us the serenity we crave nor do they bring us peace. Often, we forge our identity by defining ourselves in opposition to others, by who we are not, rather than who we are.

As the author Douglas Murray pointed out, this can lead to conflict and confusion. He writes that "while racial equality, minority rights and women's rights are among the best products of liberalism, they make the most destabilising foundations. Attempting to make them the foundation is like turning a bar stool upside down and then trying to balance on top of it."

After years of political activism where she was sure of who she was and what she wanted to achieve, Maya felt lost. "At first," she said, "I just thought I was getting older and the feeling would pass but it didn't. It was like everything I'd fought for was no longer enough. There was something missing."

Maya's problem was that she lacked a connection to God. There is no earthly identity that can make us feel complete. On the contrary, the further we step away from God, the more distant from ourselves we become and that is what the Psalmist wants to teach us.

Only God knows the inner workings of our hearts and only He can heal our deepest wounds. By finding our connection to God, we find who we really are. This knowledge was profoundly healing for Maya who went back to the faith of her childhood with renewed energy and conviction.

As for myself, I am a husband, a father, a grandfather and a pastor. Most fundamental of all, I am a child of God and that is the core of who I am. It is what gives me the strength to be the best I can be to my family, my friends and those I counsel. I know I am human and I will fall short from time to time, but I have faith that God will search my heart and forgive whatever He finds there.

That faith is who we all are, if we have the will to cast off the veil that blinds us and see God in all His glory.

And he took the children in his arms, placed his hands on them and blessed them.

(Mark 10:16)

Day 35

What can I do to make the world safer for our children?

I was speaking to Julian over dinner. He was young and had just welcomed his first child, William, into the world.

"How are you finding being a Dad?" I asked him.

"It's everything my friends prepared me for," he replied. "William cries a lot, I don't get any sleep, our social life has disappeared and I'm trying to persuade my parents to move closer to us. Other than that, it's great!"

I wasn't sure what to say next, so Julian helped me out:

"You know I'm only joking," he said, before adding, "We all know how life-changing a new baby can be but there's one feeling no-one prepared me for: as soon as William was born, I knew that I would happily give my life for him. I don't know where that feeling came from. It just appeared."

"Let the little children come to me," Jesus said and they came. Jesus always stood up for the weak and the vulnerable and he saw our ability to love our children as a mirror of God's love for us. Yet many children don't enjoy the devotion that God shows us or that Julian showed to his son.

Too many children grow up wounded by their parents or those into whose care they have been entrusted. When I was in the Far East, I remember someone telling me that children are like rice paper and we should be mindful of the mark we leave on them.

But all too often we are careless with our children. We leave marks that scar them for life and we do so because someone left a mark on us when we were children. As the Swiss educator Heinrich Pestalozzi said, "You can drive the devil out of your garden but you will find him again in the garden of your son."

If we want to make the world safer for our children, we must do as Jesus taught us and that is to be kind to all children, beginning with the child we once were, whom we carry with us every moment of our lives.

We must not allow our children to lose hope and meaning in their lives. It used to be said that "children should be seen and not heard" but Jesus taught us to live like children so that we may be open to his teaching. It is this voice of innocence we need to hear.

> *For I will pour water on the thirsty land, and streams on the dry ground; I will pour out my Spirit on your offspring, and my blessing on your descendants.*
>
> (Isaiah 44:3)

Day 36

How can I stop feeling negative?

There are many reasons we give ourselves to be angry and negative about our lives. We may feel undervalued by those closest to us or we may have been betrayed by someone we trusted. Perhaps we feel we didn't get the rewards our efforts deserve or we suffered a great injustice that left a deep wound in our hearts.

Timothy was a gifted musician in the church who found himself in a spiral of negativity after his young baby suffered cot death. "We don't deserve this," he cried, "and I don't know why God let it happen."

The night his baby died, against the wishes of his wife, he'd refused to have the little one in their bedroom. Consumed with guilt and rage, he left the church and his marriage collapsed.

God, however, does not want us to live in bitterness and negativity. He wants us to live lives blessed with hope and the redemptive power of His love.

And that is the message of the Book of Isaiah.

God knows our faith will be tested just like he tested the people of Israel. He passed a harsh judgement upon them only to remind them that He was also their salvation.

God wants us to know that we have no reason to be fearful or negative. He is with us even in our darkest moments. What He asks of us is to keep the faith. He has a purpose for us all and sometimes, when we are in difficulty, we can rediscover that purpose.

After pulling away from God, Timothy realised that his illness was an opportunity to deepen and renew his faith. In the course of his treatment, he met many people suffering like him. Inspired by their quiet courage, he realised that we all suffer and it is our duty to make sense of that suffering by keeping our faith.

In the Book of Isaiah, where God says, "I am the First and I am the Last; besides me there is no God (Isaiah 44:6), God is telling us that He, and only He, is with us in times of happiness and times of hardship.

Timothy never found his way back to God. His pain blinded him to the fact that through Jesus Christ, God shares our suffering and God is able to restore us, if only we will come to Him in our nakedness and our emptiness and let him clothe and renew us.

> *I press on toward the goal to win the prize for which God has called me heavenward in Christ Jesus.*
>
> **(Philippians 3:14)**

Day 37

What does the future hold for me?

The future is uncertain.

As we move forward with our lives, our hopes and fears travel with us. We want what's best for ourselves, our families and the community of which we are a part, but there are many things we can't control. We're told to set ourselves personal and professional goals yet it's easy to be knocked off course and sink into despair, which is what happened to Jeff.

A career-driven man in his late thirties, Jeff had always liked a drink. He prided himself on setting goals and achieving them, whether these were personal fitness goals or sales targets for his business.

But when Jeff's business folded and he experienced major failure for the first time, his drinking quickly got out of control.

"I couldn't cope," he said. "All my life I was always the one in control and then everything fell apart and I didn't know what to do. For me, the future had always been rosy, then it turned very, very dark."

Many of us feel, like Jeff, that we are in control of our lives but we are not. God is in control and what Paul is asking us to do in Philippians is to re-evaluate our goals.

At any moment, our lives can be turned upside down by a random event or a sudden change in fortune. What God wants us to know is when we put our faith in Him, our earthly future may be full of uncertainty but our eternal future is guaranteed. That is His promise to us.

Jeff recovered from his alcoholism by finding a path to God and he recited this well-known prayer every day:

"God, grant me the serenity to accept that which cannot be changed; courage to change that which can, and wisdom to know the difference, through Jesus Christ our Lord, Amen."

And the one thing that never changes is God's active interest in our lives. He wants the best for us and if our goal for the future is to be open to receiving that love, we will never lose direction in our lives.

> *As they were going down to the edge of town, Samuel said to Saul, 'Tell the servant to go on ahead of us' and the servant did so, 'but you stay here for a while, so that I may give you a message from God.'*
>
> (1 Samuel 9:27)

Day 38

What can I do when I lose focus on what matters most?

We're all busy, all the time. Or so it seems.

Attention is a scarce resource and we only have so much of it to give. With the world becoming increasingly complex and more than 90% of the world's information produced in just the last 2 years, it's little wonder that we struggle to focus on what matters.

"I lost sight of everything that was important to me," Anne told me. "I felt constantly depleted. I was inefficient at work and too tired to cope when I came home. I think they call it 'burn-out syndrome' but giving it a name didn't help my two daughters who wanted their bright, energetic Mum back."

Saul faced the same challenge of learning how to focus on what mattered when Kish, his father, lost three donkeys and he sent Saul to find them. Saul travelled to the lands of many tribes but the donkeys were nowhere to be seen.

In desperation, Saul went to see the prophet Samuel to ask if he knew where the donkeys were. When they met, Samuel told him to stop searching because the donkeys were found, to "stay here for a while, so that I may give you a message from God". It was then that Saul learned he was to be anointed King of Israel.

To focus on what matters we have to free our minds from distractions. Anne was too busy running around to focus on her daughters and on God. Saul was too busy chasing donkeys to discover the plans God had for him.

The solution for both of them was the same: to create a space in their busy lives to hear God's word. That's how Saul became King and how Anne reconnected with the church. In that way, they both learned the greatest treasure is to focus on what matters most, which is the plan God has for us all.

Be kind and compassionate to one another, forgiving each other, just as in Christ God forgave you.

(Ephesians 4:32)

Day 39

How can I forgive those who hurt me?

There is not a one of us who hasn't, at some point in our lives, been hurt by the actions of someone else.

We may have been punished or imprisoned for a crime we did not commit. Many of us have been insulted, or even physically attacked, because of our beliefs. We may also have seen those we love suffer unjustly through the malice or carelessness of others.

In such situations it is hard to forgive and forgiveness was the challenge facing the Rwandan writer Immaculee Ilibagiza after her family was slaughtered during the Rwandan genocide in 1994.

In less than a 100 days more than one million people were killed. Immaculee survived by hiding, with seven other women, in a bathroom that measured 12 square feet.

After the genocide was over, Immaculee had the opportunity to exact revenge. Felicien, the man who'd butchered her family, was captured, dragged from his prison cell and thrown at her feet.

Felicien, whose children Immaculee had played with when she was a child, couldn't lift his eyes off the ground to look at her.

The guard told Immaculee she could humiliate or hurt her family's killer in any way she wished without fear of punishment. Looking at the degraded man, now the victim of his victim, she touched his hands gently and said, "I forgive you."

Forgiveness is the heart of Jesus' message. He taught that "if anyone slaps you on the right cheek, turn to him the other also." (Matthew 5:39). By doing this, we free ourselves from the burden of carrying resentment and anger at those who have done us an injustice.

In her account of the genocide, Immaculee wrote that Felicien "had let the devil enter his heart, and the evil ruined his life like a cancer in his soul." When offered the opportunity to take "an eye for an eye and a tooth for a tooth", she replied that "forgiveness is all I have to offer." a time when we see our communities breaking apart in deepening cycles of accusation and retribution based on political allegiance, race or gender, we need, more than ever, to embrace the compassion of Jesus Christ, who made the ultimate sacrifice so that we may learn the value of forgiveness.

> *The Lord said to Moses, 'Tell the Israelites to bring me an offering. You are to receive the offering for me from everyone whose heart prompts them to give.'*
>
> **(Exodus 25:2)**

Day 40

What can I give to others when I can barely provide for my family?

Every life faces hardship.

We may be victims of exceptional events such as war, plague or natural disasters, but it is more likely that we are faced with the ordinary hardships that everyone has to deal with: financial difficulty, illness, death and injustice.

Yet, despite our circumstances, God commands us to give to Him and to others. For many of us, this makes us question what God is asking of us when He can see how we struggle to give to those close to us.

This was how Elizabeth felt when her mother, who suffered from dementia, came to live with her.

Despite the demands her mother's illness placed upon her, Elizabeth kept giving to the church community. There were times when she felt overwhelmed, yet she knew that God wanted her to maintain a generous heart, regardless of her own difficulties.

"God was reminding me," she said, "that giving of oneself is like sowing good seed and it always reaps a good harvest."

In the Gospel of Luke, Jesus says, "Give and it will be given to you" (Luke 6:38) and when he feeds five thousand people from five loaves and two fish, Jesus is reminding us that our lives are full of abundance if only we choose to see it.

When, as in Exodus, God asks us to make an offering, he is not concerned with what the offering is. What matters to God is that we give from the heart.

There were times when caring for her mother left Elizabeth exhausted. On a day when she felt guilty that she was not doing more, I said to her, "You can only give in the best way you can and God understands your tiredness." In looking at what God was asking her to give in this light, the burden of guilt vanished.

When we realise that what matters to God is that we give willingly, irrespective of our means, and that we do so without expectation of material reward, then we will gain the gift of His love, in this life and the next.

> *Then Mary took about a pint of pure nard, an expensive perfume; she poured it on Jesus' feet and wiped his feet with her hair. And the house was filled with the fragrance of perfume.*
>
> (John 12:3)

Day 41

How much does God expect me to give?

This passage from the Gospel of John takes place a week before the crucifixion. In a remarkable act of humility, Mary anoints the feet, not the head, of Jesus and she does so with an "expensive perfume" before using her hair to wipe it away.

John wants us to understand that Mary is both humble and extravagant at the same time. For many of us, it's hard to know how much and to whom we should give and this was the dilemma faced by Michael.

By nature a humble man of modest means, Michael gave what he could to the Church and served in the community as best as his ailing health allowed him to do.

Despite this generosity, Michael felt he was never giving enough.

"People tell me I give a lot," he said to me, "but that's not how I feel. I always think I can do more and I feel constantly that I'm never good enough in God's eyes."

The oil Mary poured on Jesus' feet would have cost the equivalent of a year's wages, yet it is the symbolic meaning of the act that John wants us to understand. The oil mirrored the blessings that Jesus pours into our lives: the fragrance that filled the house was the fragrance of a consecrated life.

In using her hair to clean Jesus' feet, Mary gave the most valuable gift she could give to herself and to Jesus, the gift of surrender.

And that is what God asks us to do. We may not have the money to buy extravagant gifts to give to God or to our fellow men and women. But we all have the ability to devote our lives to God.

Michael made peace with himself when he realised that every time he gave of himself he was giving exactly what God wanted him to give.

It is, then, in our many small acts of kindness and generosity that we bear witness to the sacrifice that Jesus made for us and those acts, however small they may seem, are always sufficient in God's eyes.

Through you we push back our enemies; through your name we trample our foes.

(Psalm 44:5)

Day 42

Where is God when I feel defeated?

There are many ways in which we can feel defeated.

All of us will experience many losses in the course of a lifetime as those we love, our friends and family, struggle with illness and pass away. There will be other losses, too, as our career doesn't follow the path we had hoped for or our businesses struggle financially.

For most of us, life feels like a succession of failures punctuated by the occasional success and it is tempting to ask: where is God when I feel defeated?

This is the question Marc asked as he saw his life unravel. His 15-year old daughter was taken ill and as Marc struggled to sustain his focus on his work, he was made redundant.

One night, his wife woke up and noticed he was not beside her. She called his name and he didn't answer. When she wandered downstairs she found him kneeling on the floor saying over and over again, "If you are real God, please show yourself now…"

Like all of us who devote our lives to God, Marc was familiar with the many Biblical stories where God intervenes on the side of the faithful and he struggled to understand why God had abandoned him in his hour of need.

By the time Marc spoke to me, he had all but lost his faith.

I reminded him that God never loses interest in our lives and there are many ways in which we can understand His interventions. In Psalm 44, the image of trampling our enemies suggests that God acts like a stampeding animal to ensure our triumph in any challenge we face.

Yet, God is more subtle than that. He knows that the biggest enemy we face is ourselves. When things don't go to plan, we fall into doubt and despair and because we suffer.

God sacrificed His only son, to show us all that we have a way out of suffering. We cannot avoid pain but we can experience it through faith, through the knowledge that God is with us even if it feels He is absent.

In faith, we cannot be defeated and once he realised that the enemy he had to trample was himself, Marc regained the strength to face the battles we must all, in our own way, confront.

> *I keep asking the God of our Lord Jesus Christ, the glorious Father, may give you the Spirit of wisdom and revelation, so that you may know him better.*
>
> (Ephesians 1:17)

Day 43

How can I get to know God better and gain wisdom and understanding?

It is human nature to doubt.

Advances in science and medicine are made possible by a new generation of researchers questioning the accepted truths of their predecessors and adapting those truths in the light of new discoveries.

In society and culture, children question the values of their parents, the young question the beliefs of the old, until it seems there is nothing that can withstand the ravages of doubt, including our faith in God.

Some years ago, while working in Africa, I had the privilege to spend time with Jeffrey, a leading professor and theologian who devoted his life to spreading the Gospel.

One night as we walked through the jungle, the sounds of wildlife echoing through the darkness, he turned to me and said, "Alan, how do you recognise God's voice? I know I'm a leader in the church but sometimes I feel I can't hear Him."

We both stopped in our tracks.

"All I can say Jeffrey," I said, "is that you work so hard, preparing sermons and communicating to those who reach out to you that you don't pause to hear God. People make so many demands on your wisdom, you don't take the space to stop and reflect on the wisdom of God."

Immediately Jeffrey understood and laughed when I added, "The main reason I know when God speaks is that I'm not clever enough to speak as I do without His help."

I was also reminded of the words of the hymn Dear Lord and Father of Mankind, which ends with the famous verse:

Breathe through the heats of our desire
Thy coolness and thy balm;
Let sense be dumb, let flesh retire;
Speak through the earthquake, wind, and fire,
O still small voice of calm!

If we expect God to shout loudest, to yell about His presence in our lives, we will be disappointed at our inability to hear Him.

God's voice is not loud and blaring. It is insistent and humble.

Unlike beliefs and values which change from one generation to the next, God's voice is constant. His wisdom is eternal and when we pause in the fury of our lives, that's when we will hear him and be nourished and renewed by His still, small voice of calm.

> *And He said to me, 'Son of man, stand up on your feet and I will speak to you.'*
>
> (Ezekiel 2:1)

Day 44

How can I stand strong when I feel weak?

The prophet Ezekiel is addressed by God as "Son of man," because God sees him as a representative of humanity.

Yet, despite the prophet's status, God will only speak to him if he stands on his feet. What God is telling Ezekiel is that he must resist the temptation to become a victim, to be overwhelmed by the challenges of his life or blame others for the difficulties he faces.

Sean, a long-serving and generous member of the church, discovered how hard it is to stand strong when there is so much to weaken us.

For years he had counselled those in need only to find himself brought to his knees by the loss of his wife in a car accident caused by a drunk driver. Unable to bear the injustice and randomness of the loss, he cursed the driver and when that did little to assuage his anger, he blamed God.

"God tells us to stand strong in our faith," he cried, "and I have served him faithfully for many years but how I be strong after this?"

When God demands that Ezekiel "stand up", he is demanding of us all that we refuse to live like victims, that we take ownership of our own lives and all the good and bad things that happen in them.

The psychologist Jordan Peterson writes that "to stand up straight with your shoulders back is to accept the terrible responsibility of life, with eyes wide open...It means willingly undertaking the sacrifices necessary to generate a productive and meaningful reality (it means acting to please God, in the ancient language)."

Only when we stand up can we please God. He will not receive us unless we actively take responsibility for our lives.

Think of the worst, most unjust thing that has ever happened to you and own it. Think of the cruelty of others and own it. Unless we do this, we will forever be prisoners of those who have hurt us.

We can only be free to receive and serve God when we stand up and say, 'Here I am! Accept me, O Lord, for I willingly bear the burden of my life, which gives me the strength to turn to You for salvation.'

> *Unlike the culture around you always dragging you down to its level of immaturity, God brings the best out of you, develops well-formed maturity in you.*
>
> (Romans 12:2)

Day 45

What can I really control?

There seems little we can control in our lives.

From the unreasonable behaviour of other people to sudden illness and injustice, our events feel beyond our control.

The result is we lose the balance of our minds as the loss of control leads to feelings of helplessness and despair.

Residents in a care home were given a plant to place in their rooms. Half of the residents were told to look after the plant themselves, while the other half had the plant cared for by staff. Over time, those who looked after the plant themselves were twice as likely to live as those who had no control over when and how the plant was cared for.

Joanne was a young woman whose life was out of control.

She was homeless and married to Derek who often beat her, leaving her face cut and bruised. They lived in a shelter and he never let her out of his sight until one day, Joanne turned up without her husband.

Paul, a worker at the shelter, asked her where her husband was. Joanne explained he'd been put in prison after he beat up a man so badly, his face was not recognisable.

"So what are you going to do now?" Paul asked Joanne.

"I'll wait for him," she replied. "He's my man, isn't he?"

"Well, I'll say this only once," Paul replied, "The first time you get hit you're a victim. Every time after that you're a partner. So, if you want to get beaten up again, perhaps even killed, you wait for him. But if you want to be free, then take responsibility for the situation you're in and make a change now. You can't control your husband but you have the power to change your life."

If we are to thrive, we must have the maturity to take control of our own minds and learn to love from the centre of who we are. Whether we free our lives by having faith in God is a choice. He is there waiting for us, but it is up to us to take ownership of what happens in our lives. Only then can surrender ourselves to God and be reborn.

> *No one will be able to stand against you all the days of your life. As I was with Moses, so I will be with you; I will never leave you nor forsake you.*
>
> (Joshua 1:5)

Day 46

Who will carry me when I stumble?

Words are cheap.

Promises are made then broken. Commitments are entered into only to be betrayed. Oaths of loyalty are sworn only to be discarded at the first sign of trouble.

Many of us have, at some point in our lives, felt let down by the actions of someone we trusted and this is what happened to Jenny when she discovered her husband of 20 years had been having an affair.

Despite trying to explain that he still loved her, Jenny asked her husband to leave their home. "I was more than devastated," she said. "I believe marriage is sacred and I thought my husband did too. It made me question everything. I went through all the years of our marriage and the living words he'd said, birthday and Christmas cards he'd given me, and I doubted it all. How could I be sure that the whole thing was a lie?"

We can talk about love but it is how we act that matters. We can talk about the value of fidelity but it is actually being faithful, day after day, that matters. A bond of trust, once broken, is difficult to repair.

In the well-known poem, Footprints, a man had a dream that he was walking along a beach with God beside him. When he looked back along the oat they had taken, he noticed that when he was at his saddest, there was only one set of footprints so he asked God, "Why, when I needed you most, would you leave me?" God replied, "I would never leave you. During your times of trial and suffering, when you see only one set of footprints, it was then that I carried you."

The message that God gives Joshua is that He will never forsake him. God's love never falters. He keeps His promises and honours His commitments.

It's easy to forget how strong God's commitment is to us but when we stumble, the everlasting arms are always there to catch us. God never gives up on us if we trust in Him.

> "Consider him who endured such opposition from sinners, so that you will not grow weary and lose heart.
>
> (Hebrews 1:3)

Day 47

Should I ever give up?

We are often taught that those who achieve their goals in life, do so because of persistence: where other people falter, they keep going.

The philosopher William James wrote that "the human individual lives usually far within his limits; he possesses powers of various sorts which he habitually fails to use. He energizes below his maximum, and he behaves below his optimum."

We are told the reason for this failure is our lack of grit. As the psychologist Angela Duckworth wrote, "Enthusiasm is common. Endurance is rare."

If we fail, then, the temptation is to blame our lack of persistence. This can lead to feelings of guilt and lack of self-worth, which is what Terry felt when he failed to achieve a career goal he'd promised himself he'd reach before the age of 40.

"I felt washed out," he said. "I worked so hard for so long, I focused totally on my career, I sacrificed so much and I still didn't get what I wanted."

The challenge Terry faced is one we all face. When our ambitions are dependent on other people, such as someone giving us a promotion, then we become hostages of fortune. While we can control our own thoughts and feelings, we can't control other people.

If, despite these limits to what we can control, we charge blindly forward then a few will succeed. Those are the ones whose stories we read about in self-help books. For most people, persistence in one area of our lives means we sacrifice happiness in others: the man, like Terry, who gives everything to his career may find, too late, that he is estranged from the son he neglected.

As the actor W.C. Fields said, "If at first, you don't succeed, try, try again, then quit – there's no use being a damn fool about it."

Yet we are fools.

We chase our worldly goals and fail to see that God has a different goal in mind for us. He sent his own Son to us so that we might understand that our true rewards are in Heaven and we can achieve them by being simple and constant in our faith. Even when we doubt, God will not hold it against us. He wants what's best for us and waits patiently and lovingly as we struggle our way through life.

Faith is the only human activity that brings with it the certainty of reward and the apostle Paul reminds us that "the peace of God, which transcends all understanding, will guard your hearts and your minds in Christ Jesus" (Philippians 4:6-7).

The Lord our God said to us at Horeb, 'You have stayed long enough at the mountain.'

(Deuteronomy 1:6)

Day 48

What is the secret of success?

Many of us define success in material terms.

We buy the house or the car we've always dreamed of owning and we celebrate success. We pass on this definition of success to our children and we watch as, overcome with excitement, they take their new phone or computer out of its packaging.

Yet, a few days or even moments later, the excitement has gone. Often, we feel empty, disappointed that the thing we bought to make us happy has failed to deliver on its promise.

I once watched Malcolm, a lottery winner, being interviewed. He'd won many millions of pounds and he described winning as "the best feeling I've ever had. It was like all my problems were over."

The feeling didn't last.

After the euphoria died away he said, "I no longer had a purpose. I'd given up my job but I missed having to work for a living. I bought a new car, a boat, all sorts of things, but they were meaningless."

Malcolm soon became so depressed he was unable to get up in the morning.

That is the illusion of success.

Even when we work for years so we can buy our dream home, it doesn't bring the expected fulfilment and psychologists have shown that once we are able to pay our bills, eat well and have the occasional holiday, more money makes us more anxious and less happy.

But in telling Moses that "you have stayed long enough at the mountain," isn't God saying that we can't stand still, we have to keep moving to achieve what we want? Isn't God saying we must be perpetually dissatisfied, always moving from one "mountain" to another in search of happiness?

God may be telling us to keep moving but for Him that isn't to be understood in terms of material success. He just wants us to keep learning and be active in our faith. It's not enough to let our relationship with God stop at the level of theory. God wants us to grow into His love and advance His Kingdom. To do this we have to act, which means refusing to stand still.

When we become complacent in our faith, God won't let us get stuck in a rut. He'll urge us to move on with our lives by always provoking us to greater service in His name and that is the definition of a successful life.

"
The Lord is my shepherd, I lack nothing.

(Psalm 23:1)

Day 49

How can God love me when I feel so inadequate?

There are times when we feel inadequate.

We may fail to achieve a goal we set ourselves or we become incapacitated by having a constant stream of what psychologists call Negative Automatic Thoughts.

If people have been physically or emotionally abusive towards us, we can carry the scars of that abuse for the rest of our lives. This abuse can take many forms and the scars it leaves can be invisible to anyone but the person who carries them.

This was the case with Robert.

A professionally successful and socially competent man, everyone who met him saw him as someone who could overcome almost every obstacle.

But Robert carried a secret: he believed he was average at best, useless at worst.

"It's what I'd been told almost every day as a child," he told me. "I was called a 'plodder', an 'idiot', 'stupid', all sorts of names like that. No one believed in me or that I'd ever make anything of myself."

Even when he won awards for his work, Robert's view of himself didn't change.

"I didn't believe I deserved anything," he said, "especially an award."

Like Robert, many of us destroy ourselves internally. We forge our identities out of the criticisms other people make of us, which leaves us with a deep sense of our inadequacy.

Psalm 23 provides us with a profound spiritual response to these feelings. The Psalmist reminds us that when we open our hearts to God, we "lack nothing". The struggles for self-esteem that beset us all, vanish into air as we discover a deep reserve of spiritual strength and resilience.

What gives us this strength is God's guardianship and guidance, which is the protection a shepherd gives to his flock.

Above all, God loves us because of our inadequacies not despite them. He knows we are wounded and bear the scars of the many conflicts and difficulties we face in our lives. He doesn't expect us to be perfect but nor does He want us to ruin our lives by devaluing who and what we are.

Love of self is not arrogance. When built on the foundation of the love of God and love of those who need us, it is an expression of kindness and humility.

Be still and know that I am God; I will be exalted among the nations, I will be exalted over the earth.

(Psalm 46:10)

Day 50

How can I find true rest?

We live our lives in a constant state of unease.

We worry about our finances, our jobs, our future, the future of our children and grandchildren. There seems to be an endless stream of worries that washes over us every day of our lives.

In search of an end to this unease, we chase money or give in to impulsive or addictive behaviour in that hope that it will offer us a means of escape. Too late, we realise we are chasing shadows.

Rebecca was a young woman with a troubled background. After years of going in and out of rehabilitation programmes for alcohol and substance abuse, she attempted to take her own life.

"Looking back," she said, "I was always running away from my past but however fast I ran, the past would catch up with me. So, I ran faster but all the things I was trying to run away from moved faster too and they'd always catch up with me. There was no escape. I couldn't find any rest. I was exhausted and I thought at least if I was dead, I'd be at peace. Nothing could hurt me anymore."

We rest when we take a pause in the busy-ness of our lives or take a while to sit and read in the comfort of an armchair. But there is a deeper rest than this, an equilibrium of the soul and inner tranquillity that a connection with God gives us.

Jesus says, "Come to me, all you that are weary and are carrying heavy burdens, and I will give you rest. Take my yoke upon you, and learn from me; for I am gentle and humble in heart, and you will find rest for your souls. For my yoke is easy, and my burden is light." (Matthew 11:28-30).

Rebecca eventually found salvation in Jesus. He offered her rest and she accepted the gift. For the first time in her life, she found true peace.

It's estimated that we spend up to seven years of our lives worrying about things that never happen or turn out better than we feared. This is not how Jesus wants us to live. When we believe in Him, we know that God is engaged in our lives and we need to remind ourselves of this when we feel worried or overwhelmed. He will, as Jesus said, lighten our burden.

> *And the Lord said to him, 'Therefore whoever kills Cain, vengeance shall be taken on him sevenfold.' And the Lord set a mark on Cain, lest anyone finding him should kill him.*
>
> (Genesis 4:15)

Day 51

What is wrong with taking revenge on those who hurt the ones I love?

Every one of us understands what it feels like to be hurt by another person. It may be something that has been said to us or we may have been subjected to a violent attack.

Yet, it is often worse to see those we love subjected to physical or emotional abuse. When those we love, especially our children, are hurt, we feel overwhelming anger. Swift on the heels of that anger comes the desire to strike back as we thirst for revenge.

This is how Jackie felt when Mia, her daughter, was bullied online.

For some time before she found out what was happening, Jackie noticed Mia withdrawing into herself. Mia, who used to be a bubbly teenager, would spend hours in her room and every attempt Jackie made to talk to Mia was met with silence or a tantrum.

After one particularly nasty argument, Jackie took the matter into her own hands. She accessed her daughter's social media accounts and was horrified by what she saw. As she scrolled down the screen, she read a trail of messages abusing and bullying her own daughter.

Jackie recognised the bullies. They were girls from Mia's school.

Jackie felt a rage she didn't think she was capable of and her first impulse was to go to these girls' homes and break the door down.

When we are faced with this irresistible impulse for revenge, we should learn from the mark God placed on Cain to protect him against revenge attacks for the killing of his brother. The reason God did this was because He knew what happens when human beings take the law into their own hands. If God had allowed vengeance to be taken against Cain, then the descendants of Cain would exact vengeance in response and the cycle would escalate endlessly.

God protected Cain because it was His responsibility, not ours, to judge and punish. He is asking us to have faith in His wisdom and to refrain from violence.

After a few sleepless nights consumed by anger, Jackie prayed for guidance. When she felt God had answered her prayers, she spoke to Mia. Together they learned about how to deal with online bullies. Gradually, Mia grew stronger and the abuse slowed down then stopped.

It takes courage and faith to show restraint. God knows that if we take the law into our own hands, the violence will never end, which is why, in Paul's Letter to the Romans, we read: "Vengeance is mine, says the Lord. I will repay" (Romans 12:19).

> *On coming to the house, they saw the child with his mother Mary, and they bowed down and worshiped him. Then they opened their treasures and presented him with gifts of gold, frankincense and myrrh.*
>
> (Matthew 2:11)

Day 52

Where was God when I lost my unborn baby?

The Bible has many stories of women giving birth after believing they would die childless.

Sara, Abraham's wife, gave birth to Isaac despite being "barren." Isaac married Rebecca and "prayed to Jehovah for his wife who was barren." She, too, gave birth as did Rachel, wife of Jacob, Ana, wife of Elcana and Elisabeth, wife of Zacharias, all of whom believed they could never bring a child into the world.

In these stories, God is reminding us that every birth is a miracle and the greatest miracle of them all is the birth of Jesus to the virgin Mary.

Yet, not all women can give birth while others, like Allison, lose their baby during pregnancy.

I spoke to Allison a few days after her miscarriage. Having been told that she and her husband could never have children, she'd been blessed with the miracle of a baby only to miscarry early in the pregnancy.

"What have I done to deserve this?" she asked me. "My husband and I called our baby 'our little miracle' but it wasn't a miracle was it?"

I remember once talking to a carpenter who was upset having finished making a small, wooden coffin to carry the body of his friend's baby who'd died suddenly. It's wrong," he said, "that one so small should die." Over the years, with God's help, I have supported women who lost their babies and I feel what the carpenter felt. It feels so harsh.

In the Nativity and the stories of miraculous birth, God is letting us know that He can make the impossible possible. He enters into the despair of childlessness and brings the joy of new life against all odds. Yet, He also wants us to know that He sent His son to heal the wounds of those who cannot conceive children or who suffer the trauma of miscarriage.

The miracle of Jesus' birth gives us a message that anything is possible. The manner of his death gives us hope that, even when the miracle we prayed for in this life doesn't happen, the biggest miracle of all, the gift of eternal life, awaits us in the next.

In dying to redeem us, Jesus opened the gates of Heaven to all our children, even those who cannot be born.

• One Community • One Ministry • A Worldwide Impact

About Lifelink Global

Lifelink Global holds to the God-given principle that He commanded us to engage with society, not to withdraw from it.

Every member of the Community, be they an individual or a Church, plays their part in serving God by building a community united in their passion for Christ and their compassion for the world.

The shared Apostolic Ministry of our Community is to:

> Spread the Gospel of the Kingdom to every man, woman and child in every Nation on Earth
>
> Train and equip future Leaders to lead our churches and our worldwide mission, Now and Always
>
> Dedicate our lives to serving God and relieving the suffering of our fellow men and women in His name

We are united by:

> A Passion for Jesus
>
> Devotion to the Kingdom of God
>
> Compassion for the lost, lonely and dispossessed

www.lifelink.global

www.ingramcontent.com/pod-product-compliance
Lightning Source LLC
Chambersburg PA
CBHW071527080526
44588CB00011B/1584